# THE
# MYSTERY
# OF
# CHRIST

*Foreword by Zinovya Dushkova*

# THE
# MYSTERY
# OF
# CHRIST

## The Life-Changing Revelation
## of the Great Initiate

## THALES OF ARGOS

*Translated from the Russian by*
*Alexander Gerasimchuk with John Woodsworth*

**Radiant Books**
Sheridan, Wyoming

Library of Congress Control Number: 2021913519

First English Edition
published in 2021 by Radiant Books,
an imprint of Dushkova Publishing LLC
www.radiantbooks.org

ISBN 978-1-63994-000-4 (hardback)
ISBN 978-1-63994-001-1 (paperback)
ISBN 978-1-63994-002-8 (e-book)

# Contents

## *Foreword*
### by Zinovya Dushkova

IN THE WORLD there exist so many books that have been written for a variety of reasons, and most of them have been published out of material considerations. But there are some works which cannot be placed on a par with those that carry a purely informational load. They are more on the plane of perishable, transitory "values," which can disappear from the pages of the Earth's history without leaving a trace.

One book that bears such eternal and imperishable values within itself is *The Mystery of Christ*, which, it may be said, has paved its own path. And it was born in the period after the 1917 Russian revolution in the city of Odessa, Ukraine — the home of those who were destined to peer into the Annals of Eternity and to revive, before the eyes of human masses, fragments of life that initially occurred on the nascent continents of our planet, as well as to reveal — as the crowning passage of the narrative — those direful events associated with the Name of Jesus Christ.

One can perceive in different ways the story expounded by George Osipovich Volsky and Anastasia Vasilievna Theodoridi, but as is known, Truth invariably goes through three stages: "This cannot be," "There is something in this," and "Who doesn't know this!" I hope you, dear reader, will treat everything you read here with great attention, without descending to the position of denial, and for a start, at least, you will try to see that "there is something in this"!

The book has traversed a very difficult path in the form of individual chapters, often copied by those who were attempting to pave for themselves the thorny ways leading to the diamond peaks of Truth. Through unknown paths in Ukraine, the Baltic states, and Russia, getting into Romania and from there into France and Germany, its scattered parts have continued their movement forward and embraced an ever greater number of minds and souls, showing the ability to "assimilate the unassimilable."

Thus, the mysterious character named Thales of Argos has continued to excite the minds and disturb the human souls who try to learn about him as much as possible. And many have associated him with the image of Thales of Miletus, who is regarded as the "father of philosophy" and the founder of Greek culture and statehood. His numerous discoveries in the domains of astronomy and mathematics, cosmogony and cosmology, physics and biology, geography and meteorology, are considered by many researchers as fundamental to the development of European science.

It should be noted that the main tenet of the Teaching of Thales is that the first fundamental principle of all that exists is *water*. It is impossible to disagree with this, especially for those seekers who have come nearer to solving the Mystery of the interaction of Cosmic Waters with the Earth's water masses. And although the date of Thales' birth takes us to a time several centuries before Christ, nevertheless, when we proceed from the principle of reincarnation of the soul, those who advance along the path of comprehending Truth should not exclude the possibility of his meeting with Christ Jesus. Undoubtedly, the image of this, more than the mysterious personality of the ancient Greek scientist and philosopher, even through the ages, continues to agitate minds — for confirmation we need only turn to the works of some historians of the 19th and 20th centuries.

And so, after many centuries, a question arises before us: Is *he* or not *he* — Thales, the Great Initiate of the Theban Sanctuary, who, after appearing before Christ Jesus, to His question, "Will you follow Me as well?" replied: "I cannot *but* follow Thee — however, I can never follow those who follow Thee..."

And here we shall not sin against Truth, if we answer: yes and no, inasmuch as the physical flesh of Thales of Miletus, steeped in a multitude of legends, had passed through a number of transmutations; this is thanks to his possession of secret knowledge, part of which became the property of those around him. No mortal on the Earth is able to know from what Cosmic depths his Stellar Spirit came into the Solar System, for what purpose and with what tasks. Or how many bodies he can recreate through the division of his Spirit — bodies willing to carry out Labour in different parts of the world. Will he be amidst the thick of human masses in a state of the utmost density or infinite rarefaction — or will he carry out unknown Deeds at the level of Ethereal Spheres?

Humanity can judge merely within the framework of a certain visible plane, while the whole Truth will be hidden from the eyes of the uninitiated. And most often it happens that the Spirit remains in other spheres of habitation and forms only the quaternary of bodies of its septenary structure in order to test how successful it will be in terms of aspiration towards spiritual and eternal values. In this way the human flesh undergoes a number of tests, being exposed to alchemical influence at the deep cellular level.

And Thales of Miletus experiences the entire process of mystical transfiguration, when his perishable elements acquire imperishable properties. The Spirit is immortal! The human body is mortal... However, the eternal quest for immortality has lasted from the beginning of the world's creation, and here the gaze of many seekers of Truth has turned in the direction of elemental forces.

At different times, different elements have been considered as the first fundamental principle of matter from which life on the Earth originated. And here one should not "butt the heads" of those who singled out one of the elemental forces, for all of them were subject to Cosmic Laws that intended them to play a major role at a certain period of Time. Thales of Miletus enshrined on a pedestal the element of water, perceiving it as primary matter, and herein lies a special sense — a Cosmic sense... He came back to the *terra firma* of the Earth, which, it may be said, he never left!..

Thales of Argos came in the Spirit, and at the same time in the body. What does this mean? It means that the element of Water is called upon for the Great Co-operation with the element of Fire, for a dangerous time has arrived when a powerful Force field is created, and at the opposite poles are the Spirit and the body, or in other words: the Heavenly Forces and the earthly forces. The physical human body, being a part of the quaternary, as is known, consists of 50–80% water (depending on age), while the higher triad contains mostly elements with fiery properties. With age, a person loses liquid, and it is especially good if the water that has managed to absorb certain qualities of spirituality also manifests the ability to crystallize the stellar light within itself, tilting the pan of the Scales in favour of the higher Divine triad. Thus, in order to help the Human Race establish at the level of all its sevenfold structures the balance of the Karmic Scales, certain Great Initiates need to be dissolved in the mass of creations of the planet Earth which remain ignorant of the Distant Worlds patronizing them.

And what about George Volsky and Anastasia Theodoridi? Who are they and what was their true role which they were called upon to play by extracting — from the Akashic Records and from the memories of their own hearts — all those scenes of Life that have occurred from the beginning of the origin of humanity? And how did people treat those who brought them the Light of Salvation, thereby endowing the entire sublunary world with boundless Love? Alas, the retrospective is all too obvious. History repeats itself, revealing the images of those who committed betrayals, tortures, crucifixions... And, nevertheless, the Great Sowing of the seeds of Cosmic Love has been carried on from age to age!

To Volsky and Theodoridi, who in the distant past received a certain degree of Initiation in the Theban Sanctuary and who managed to revive the gift of insight within themselves, was given the opportunity to *become*, but not to *be*, the one through whose eyes they would look into the Past — through the eyes of Thales of Argos (otherwise known as Argive). The Fiery Ray of the Spirit of the Great Initiate literally pierced their hearts, submerging them in the arms of the supreme imperishable structures that preserved the formula of those currents which were generated at the moment of the meeting of Thales of Argos with Christ Jesus in the garden of Magdala.

So, some believe that Volsky was Thales, but to *become* and to *be* — these are two completely different concepts that rest on the energy level. Only Thales can *be* Thales; however, to *become* him for a certain period of time is possible for someone whom he deems necessary to initiate by his own currents, in which the dominant note of his sound will be discernible. And such a person could only be one who has reached a particular level of Initiation. The body is merely a "vessel," a garment which does not represent the essence of its contents, and this applies to many dwellers of the Earth.

However, the life of the Initiates proceeds, as a rule, according to other Laws. And the flesh of an Initiate can sometimes serve as a haven for another Spirit, who needs to solve a specific task. Everything is subject to the Law of Expediency, and wasting valuable time on the incarnation, or the maturing of the soul, and so on, is too costly in terms of energy, and therefore the energy-saving mode is the most acceptable on the Path requiring lightning-speed advancement.

Thus, in the beginning it may only be a temporary vessel that demonstrates the ability to accept smaller vibrational constants of the Ray of another Spirit. And as crystallization occurs, the vessel acquires more than 51% of the currents of another Individuality. This now allows speaking about a different name — the name of the one whom this vessel has *become*.

In connection with the aforesaid, Argive, upon receiving the higher frequency support, was able to imbue with the Fires of his own Ray more than 51% of the subtle structures of Volsky, who thus managed to *become* — and, for a certain period of time, to *be* — Thales of Argos. But, of course, he was not the 100% Thales of Argos, for, as has already been said, only Thales can be himself.

The same also applies to Theodoridi, whose image is associated with the Sicilian philosopher, physician, priest, and prophet — Empedocles. In the distant past he developed the Teaching of the transmigration of souls, which was based on the concept of "four elements" that form the roots of things: fire, air, water, and earth — elemental forces which are spread in the human blood. And blood is an intermediate substance between the subtle and the dense body. And although it circulates through the veins and arteries and water constitutes almost 90% of the blood plasma, it nevertheless carries within itself certain elements of fiery property.

Empedocles himself repeatedly said that he was previously incarnated in both male and female bodies, and even in the form of birds... The world of the Earth is binary, and, of course, in order to maintain the balance, reincarnations are necessary — even in the case when the Spirit is called upon to bring into the world, solely, either the currents of the Great Masculine Principle or those of the Feminine. However, as an experiment, the Spirit of an Initiate is able to create simultaneously male and female bodies, uniting them with the aim of accomplishing a specific mission.

Empedocles was the closest to the currents of Thales and he could transmit the greatest constants. Therefore, only he could prepare the subtle structures of Volsky and Theodoridi, endowing them with his basic fires, upon which the immensely increased Fires of the Individuality of Thales of Argos could then rely. In other words, Volsky and Theodoridi, after succeeding in *becoming* Empedocles, were also able to *become* the "vessel" and haven for the Spirit of Thales of Argos.

Of course, for the human mind much will remain unclear, giving rise to doubts in the above-mentioned process, but as the ancient sages said: "When in doubt, abstain!" For while the secret Veil of Isis cannot be taken off completely, it can be slightly lifted — enough that the most advanced representatives of the Human Kingdom are able to perceive Truth.

Up to the present day, Thales of Argos has been a cosmic mystery for humanity. And he alone has the right to reveal it by degrees, manifesting to our gaze the pattern of his Spirit's advancement, both on the Earth and in the

Distant Worlds. After all, who but he himself can assert with certainty, in whom, and when, exactly, was hidden one of the secrets of his incarnations — associated either with the division of his Spirit or the separation of a quaternary with the aim of experimentally traversing an earthly path?!

Only God knows who we are in Eternity! While on the Earth we can be merely a partial manifestation of either our own Individuality or the Spirit which is consonant with us. Moreover, we know that, at a certain stage, a disciple renounces his own name and accepts the name of his Master.

For a more complete understanding of the mysterious Path of Thales of Argos, it should be mentioned that, over the course of many centuries after the Crucifixion of Christ, messages appeared in the world sent by this Great Initiate. Yet they remained unknown, and were preserved in the Treasury of the Theban Sanctuary. These messages were later moved to the Himalayas for a number of specific reasons, including those related to the fact that Thales of Argos left the Western Lodge, and was initiated in the Brotherhood represented by the Eastern Lodge.

Nevertheless, a letter in the Romanian language has reached us, which was delivered to readers in the city of Galați through one monk in 1943 and is now included in this edition. Of course, messages could be in different languages, since for Initiates there are no barriers to setting forth text in any given language, either by themselves or together with the help of someone whom they choose to be the "mouthpiece" of the word of Truth on the earthly plane. Many people translated texts themselves into their native tongue so as to distribute the word of the Supreme Wisdom among their friends and family. After all, the human soul, longing for its native language spoken in the infinite expanses of Eternity, eternally searches for a melody — one difficult to express in earthly terms. And this ethereal tonality can be read between the lines of books which can be classified as sacred; it can also be heard in music, in the voice of a singer...

Thus, Anastasia Theodoridi, being a famous opera singer as well as a professor at the Odessa Conservatory, left an indelible trace both in the souls of her listeners and in invisible space. She was not only a performer and teacher, but also someone who carried out alchemical work, producing in front of her audience divinely wonderful music, in which sounded the unsurpassed beauty and harmony of the Supreme Spheres. And for this it was necessary to merge both with her higher triad and with the invisible energy of her Master...

It should also be mentioned that in 1950 Theodoridi had a conversation with the Masters Morya and Koot Hoomi, who watched and assisted her in her most difficult moments. They also told her that a time of cosmic reconstruction had come...

A multitude of hues of sounds inaudible to the human ear were brought by the texts received from Above. In these Messages and Letters could be sensed a special aroma that permeated pure and child-like open souls, thanks to which people began to be transfigured at the cellular level.

The aroma of the sound of the written or spoken word is so important for the soul and stellar spirit that are longing for their Fatherly Home! Without it, the higher human triad simply suffocates; on the verge of death it receives a saving gulp of air in the form of a little message from the Empyreal World. Indeed, for many people, *The Mystery of Christ* has served — and still serves — as this elixir resurrecting them to life. In essence this book represents Apocryphal sacred messages expounded on behalf of the Great Initiate of the Theban Sanctuary to his friend Empedocles.

Again, returning to the Romanian edition of the letter of Thales of Argos, it says that "Empedocles, at the beginning of the present epoch, the seeker of the 'I' returned to you in the image of Faustus — in fact, each and every one of you are him, the people of this pivotal century, who fight with the two faces of evil." And, of course, Thales expresses not only hope, but also confidence that the human soul, acting from the invariable Core of Existence, will still return to the Realm where "golden branches are reflected in the waters of Life." Here we again find mention of water...

From time immemorial the Gods speak their own language, and people of the future must understand this language — not only at the level of the soul, but also in interpersonal communication. And the basics of this tongue should be mastered day by day through immersing oneself in reading texts from Above. And in this task the book currently presented to your attention will serve as a useful step.

The Mystery of Christ has neither beginning nor end, and here is revealed merely a "fragment" of the Great Sacrifice, yet its dimension is not comparable with anything! Almost two thousand years ago people were responsible for the most serious consequences, the results of which humanity has been reaping up to the present day. As for the pages of the earlier history, from the moment when Antarctica was a flourishing continent and where many Messengers of Distant Worlds dwelt, it should be said that all the characters mentioned in this book were resurrected again after traversing an immensely long path in human bodies.

So, along with the heroes who played a positive role, those who can be called anti-heroes also came up, since those who had committed betrayal before have continued to be traitors from century to century, and the stigma of treachery has remained an "indelible" mark on souls that continue to vibrate at the level of the Animal Kingdom. The visible and invisible characters of this "Mystery" have again returned to the Earth — some in dense bodies and some in subtle. And by the Will of the Karmic Law their pathways have begun to intersect in the present time.

And therefore the final full stop still cannot be put, for the Mystery of Christ now related to His Second Coming is just beginning to unfold, sweeping away from the stage of Life those who persecuted and tortured His Heralds as well as those who served as Forerunners at the threshold of the Great Advent of Jesus Christ in His Divine Spirit.

And the Great Initiate Thales of Argos himself has come to us as a Messenger of Pluto, in the role of a witness and an adjudicator of Comic Justice. And Pluto has been entrusted with a special mission, since it is situated in the border sphere, periodically either being inside the Solar System or venturing beyond its limits. In essence it is similar to the fragment of the Chintamani, detached from the main Stone, in this case — from another Planet-Progenitor, which is outside the boundaries of the Solar System. A long time ago, this Planet had already lost her "best daughter," who perished in a catastrophe — her fragments have formed the asteroid belt between Mars and Jupiter. And Pluto was once part of her, just as in former times Australia was part of a larger continent known as Lemuria. Pluto serves as a kind of Cosmic Scales, which weigh the whole conglomerate of accumulated currents.

One of its pans is within the Solar System, while the other is beyond its borders.

How fruitful all humanity has been in its totality, how it has affected the life activity of neighbouring planets and — most importantly — whether its contribution has been constructive or destructive in relation to the Distant Worlds?! This is the crucial factor in determining whether our planet will be admitted into the higher community, which is represented by the Sacred Planets. The last word has not yet been said either by people or by their Masters; it has not been said by either the Earth or the Sun, or, for that matter, by the network of planets surrounding them both inside and outside the Solar System...

Let us remember the repentance which emanated from the lips of one of the High Priests, Melchizedek: "For the futility of any, even the highest, earthly glory before Christ's Crown of Thorns."

We have again been given the great right to relive the Mystery of the First Coming, as well as the Second Epiphany of Christ, and therefore the Afterword awaits us ahead!..

**Zinovya Dushkova**
Author of *The Book of Secret Wisdom*
and *The Teaching of the Heart* series

# I. The Cup of the Second Initiation

*Thales of Argos —*
*to those present —*
*at the Supreme Wisdom*
*of the Eternally Young*
*Virgin-Mother — rejoice!*

NINE THOUSAND YEARS ago, the all-wise Heraclitus the Obscure spoke:

"O Thales of Argos! Your hour has come! Today, when the Holy Ra sets, you will descend into the underground temple of the Goddess Isis and will accept there the Cup of the Second Initiation from the hands of the Divine Mother. Thales of Argos! Is your soul strong? Thales of Argos! Is your heart pure? Thales of Argos! Is your mind wise? For if you lack these three qualities, O mortal, you will never withstand the gaze of the Great Goddess-Mother."

"O Teacher!" I replied to him. "My soul is strong, my heart is pure, and my mind is great. After being admitted by you, I shall descend undaunted into the underground chamber of the temple, and your disciple will not disgrace his Master."

"Go, Thales of Argos!" uttered Heraclitus.

And when twilight shadows covered the great mirror-like surface of the Nile, and night breezes began to breathe out of the desert, cooled from sultriness, I, Thales of Argos, after wrapping myself in a cloak and taking with me a lamp bearing the ignited fire of the Earth, descended into the underground temple of Isis. For a long time I walked along the narrow corridor that sometimes went down to a cleft, where I crawled on my hands and knees, without knowing whether there were an exit ahead or whether I would ever be able to get back out. I climbed damp stairs, proceeded through gigantic catacombs, water dripping from its ceiling vaults, and then... ahead of me loomed a ladder of forty-nine rungs. I ascended. There was a door edged in iron, on which I saw burning symbols signifying: "Mortal, stop!"

But I, Thales of Argos, had come for Immortality — did these warning inscriptions really matter to me?! With a firm hand I opened wide the door and entered. It smelled like the dampness of a huge underground vault. For a long time I walked forward. My steps on the flagstones rang out with a hollow echo.

Suddenly, in the heights far above my head, a light flashed, and then it became larger, wider, bluer... Quivering shadows started to run in all directions; columns, niches, statues began to take shape, and I found myself standing in the middle of a huge temple. Ahead was a simple altar, made of white marble. On it was a golden chalice, and there, behind the altar, rose a statue of a woman with her face veiled. In one hand she held a sphere, and in the other a triangle, its apex pointing down. This temple was empty: there was just me, Thales of Argos, face to face with the statue of the Goddess Isis. No sound... No rustle... Dead silence.

But here come those who have requested the Second Initiation, without knowing what to do, without knowing how to ask, without knowing how to call forth! They come here alone, only with their Wisdom, with the purity of their hearts, and the strength of their souls. And I, Thales of Argos, the wise son of light-bearing Hellas, a descendant of the royal dynasty of the City of the Golden Gates, approached the altar with bold steps. I raised my hands and imperiously summoned one who had always responded to my calls as the Lord of the Element of Air.

A light breath swept through the temple, and I heard:

"I am here, Argive! What do you want from me in this terrible place I am not at all accustomed to?"

"Help and advice," I told him. "How do I summon the Great Goddess Isis?"

"Alas, Argive, that I do not know."

"Then go away!" I commanded.

And I, Thales of Argos, was left alone with my Wisdom. I delved into my past, I remembered everything that was in the Great Atlantis. I bravely soared to the Highest Planes of Reason. I audaciously set out to fathom all the secret teachings. I knew that if I did not call the Goddess, I would never make my way out of this temple, just as those who had descended here before me had failed to escape.

But here my Wisdom prompted me to decide what to do. I boldly began to utter the Great Secret Prayers that had been heard in Atlantis, in the temple of the Eternally Young Virgin-Mother.

"O Mother Isis!" I pleaded. "Open the veil of Thy face! I know Thee! I prayed to Thee in the Great Atlantis! Lift Thy veil! I know Thee under the name of the Eternally Young Virgin-Mother! O Great Mother, open Thy veil to Thy priest!"

And slowly and quietly, from the remote corners of the temple, I could make out the quivering silvery sounds of a sistrum. Somewhere above, bright bells began to ring, and I heard some distant singing. A bluish-silvery mist started to fill the temple, and the cloud of this haze was thicker over the altar. Two eyes blazed up amidst the fog. If only you, like me, who am now approaching the boundaries of the Universe, could see the depths of the abyss of Chaos, then you would be able to get an idea of the depth of these eyes. Here is the outline of the head in a *nemes* — a countenance of ethereal beauty. Here is a gigantic torso — incomprehensible in the charm of its lines. And here are the angelic choirs... No, this is the voice of the Goddess. And I hear:

"O Argive! Great is your Wisdom! Argive, great is your audacity! Argive, great will be your reward as well! I have come to you, Argive. I have come to you, my old priest who prayed to Me in the temples of Atlantis. I have come to you now, O Great Beacon of the Theban Sanctuary, as your protectress — Isis. Come closer, My son! Let Me bestow My breath upon you."

Strong was my soul. I bravely approached the altar and knelt. And here I received the breath of the Goddess-Mother.

"O Thales of Argos!" She said to me. "In the infinity of the Universe, I appear in many forms. Yet only the wise, like you, Argive, are able to recognize Me in My endless manifestations. Argive, I knew you would recognize Me. I knew this because when you, O Wise One, while receiving the First Initiation, was talking in Hellas with My light-bearing daughter — whom you call the Goddess Pallas Athena — even then I could read in your thoughts that everything is one: the Mind which was proceeding towards the Great Revelation. It was then that I marked you with My finger. I knew that today, too, your Wisdom would remain a victor.

"What shall I reward you with, O My great son? I see your answer: 'With nothing, O Great Mother!' Yet I shall reward you with My words, Argive: Strange, incomprehensible, and unusual will be your destiny! You, a human being, will not be a human being. Your power will be unconquerable. However, you, Argive, will bring this power to... My feet. Thousands of years will pass, they will run over your head, and only then will you, who are

Great in your Wisdom, understand what I have told you in this temple."

The Goddess lifted the chalice, brought it to Her right breast, and a stream from this breast poured into the chalice. When it was full, Isis approached me.

"Drink, My son! Drink the milk of your Mother!"

And I drank it... A thunderclap rang in my chest; the roar of hundreds of thousands of Cosmoses flashed over my head, as though I were endlessly falling into the abyss, yet ever ascending to the Fiery Veil. When I woke up, I saw bending over my head the concerned but gentle face of my Master Heraclitus.

"Arise, my son! Arise, O new Beacon of the Thebes Sanctuary!"

**Thales of Argos**

## II. The Third Initiation

*Thales of Argos —*
*to those present —*
*at the Supreme Wisdom*
*of the Eternally Young*
*Virgin-Mother — rejoice!*

NOW I SHALL TELL you about my Third Initiation. Six thousand years ago, all the secret Sanctuaries of the planet Earth received a notification that the Initiates of the second degree who wished to receive the Third Initiation, should gather in a group of twelve in the Secret Hall of the White Brotherhood, to prepare for the Great Initiation.

The Great Heraclitus called me. He laid his hands on me and, while peering into my eyes with his fiery orbs, he said to me:

"Argive, my great son! Do you wish to be honoured with the Great Initiation?"

"Yes, I do," I answered.

"Argive!" Heraclitus continued, his brow now furrowed by dim features of concern, "Argive, are you ready? Remember that the trial of the Great Initiation involves terrible consequences for those who are unable to endure it. Whoever fails to withstand temptation loses everything, returns to the human herd in the form of a poor original monad and begins everything anew. Such is the punishment for pride that does not correspond to knowledge. So I ask you again: Argive, are you ready? I would not want to lose you, my beloved son, O pride of Hellas!"

"Fear not, I am ready," I replied.

Heraclitus lowered his hands.

"See, Argive, the Initiation I accepted more than a hundred thousand years ago still left much of humanity within me. I came to love you. But we cannot know our future."

"My father, I fear nothing. Let me go, and just as I did not disgrace you in the underground temple of the Goddess Isis, so I shall not disgrace you here either."

And I received the blessing of Heraclitus and set out for the Himalayas. In the underground hall of the Himalayan chambers, I was greeted by the Three: the King and Father of our planet, Melchizedek; Arraim, clad in a white cloak; and the eternally handsome Hermes. There were twelve of us, and we heard the speech of Melchizedek:

"My children! You are about to be sent for a test into another world, where you will be assigned great tasks. But there you will be left only with your own Wisdom, for the Heavens will be closed for you. The whole world will be deaf to you, and you must manage with your Wisdom alone. I talk little, my children, but you do understand me. Are you ready? Whoever feels they are unprepared, let them remain here, for death is inevitable for those who fail the test, and my fatherly heart will be flooded with tears."

We were all silent. Nobody admitted to being unready.

We were brought to a temple, where there were twelve stone beds. We were given a flavoured brew, we were enveloped in similarly fragrant charms, and, lying on these marble beds, we fell asleep in a magical dream.

When we woke up, we saw ourselves almost in the same temple, but a strange picture emerged before us: hitherto unseen windows decorated with flowers and strange paintings, an altar unlike our altar, which likewise featured some strange paintings and strange writings... We got up and walked to the windows. A wondrous spectacle appeared to our eyes: a kind of endless distances, forests of unknown hue; waters shimmering all silvery and taking on a golden hue near the shores... New aromas surrounded us and we heard some mysterious ringing — this was the ringing of flowers growing near the temple. And then the door opened, and in front of us appeared an old man, whose body was covered only with a bandage around his thighs, and he said to us:

"The King and Father of the planet asks you in."

We entered, passing through a marvellous garden, where we saw flowers we had never seen before — flowers singing and ringing; fountains were chanting, their waters emitting wonderful music. And then we came to an even more wondrous hall, erected from marble and nephrite — a hall which welcomed us with open arms. In the middle of the hall stood a throne, and on the throne was sitting a mighty man of gigantic stature, a black mane of hair flowing over his shoulders; the imperious gaze of his fiery eyes all but froze our wise souls. He rose from his throne, bowed to us, and said:

"O children of the distant Earth! I asked your leaders to send you to me. I am the King and Father of this planet, which is many times larger than your little Earth.

"Far into the Cosmos the news has spread of your Wisdom, and I have called you to help me arrange my planet. You will be teachers, you will be priests and rulers for my people. My people are kind but still wild, and you need to lead them along the path of evolution — a process which reigns everywhere on your little Earth!"

And we bowed before the King and Father...

I shall convey to you only what is most important. Work started. The King and Father of the planet had a marvellous mind: he knew everything; he seemed to penetrate the life of every blade of grass; and we, the wise ones, set zealously to work. We had become kings, we had become Great Teachers, we had become High Priests... The people had turned out to be quite receptive, but quietly so. Everyone started to work, except for one: one refused to carry out the mission of the King, refused to carry out the mission of a Great Teacher, refused to carry out the mission of a High Priest. And this one who refused was none other than me, Thales of Argos! I looked calmly into the wrathful eyes of the King and Father of the planet, and told him:

"O King and Father! In order to be a teacher for your people, I need first to come to know them. I shall not accept any mission until I study them."

The King and Father frowned.

"How much time do you need, Argive?" he asked me.

"One of our earthly years," I replied.

"And how will you explore them?" he asked me, peering at me inquisitively.

"I shall walk amidst your people, shall watch, shall question, and shall think."

"But you are a human being, and you have human needs, how will you exist?"

"O King and Father!" I answered. "You are aware that I, as an Initiate of the second degree, can survive without food for whole years at a time. But apart from that, in some small hut, will there really be not a piece of bread for a wanderer? Shall I not experience among your people a simple and noble attitude towards a wayfarer?"

"Yes, of course," the King and Father agreed, "but you have surprised me with your request and your refusal. In one year, I shall wait for you here, or otherwise I may think that you have just now decided to decline to take on the cares entrusted to you, but that you needed to do this on the Earth."

"King and Father," I said. "We thought you were wise only on your own planet, but now I see that you are also wise in earthly Wisdom, for you know everything that was done in the earthly temples of Initiates in the Himalayas."

And I left, feeling his steely gaze on the back of my head.

I passed the lands where my brothers were applying all their efforts to cast seeds of earthly Wisdom into pure, virgin hearts. The wondrous Nature illumined by two suns and three moons was truly fabulous. My comrades had become captivated by their work. They remembered the precept that they needed to merge with others: they entered into the life of the planet, they had even become husbands on this fairy planet. Women here were indescribably beautiful, and it seemed that the whole planet was permeated with heavenly bliss. It was sheer joy, and if there was one dark spot on the entire planet, it was me.

In a dark cloak, carrying a staff, I was walking along beautiful country roads, accompanied by my friends. They often asked me to visit them, invited me to spend the night in their luxury shelters, and even assumed I was dead. And so, by the end of the year, I was approaching the palace of the planet's King and Father. Dusty and unwashed, with tousled hair, I climbed the sparkling stairs of the palace. The King and Father was sitting on his throne, surrounded by a glistening retinue, including some of my friends in their magnificent garments. And I rose to my feet in front of the King and Father.

"Well, Thales of Argos, are you ready to undertake your work?"

As though a drop had fallen from a huge dome onto the marble floor in silence — so my answer resounded:

"No!"

Angrily the King and Father jumped up.

"Argive! You are signing your own death warrant: Have you forgotten that I summoned you? Think carefully!"

"I have been thinking about it for a whole year," I replied.

And then something unimaginable took place: a tired, filthy pilgrim from the Earth reached out his dirty hand and pulled a gilded chair up to the throne of the King and Father, saying to him:

"And now we'll have a talk."

The King and Father became wrathful, as though he were suffocating.

"Despicable worm, how dare you?!" he yelled.

And I quietly shook my head:

"Leave, leave this, and let me ask you a few questions. You call yourself the King and Father. Tell me, where are the Builders of this planet? Tell me, who stood at the cradle of your people? And if someone stood beside it, then he must have been sent by the Ineffable One, bless His Name! And if he was indeed sent, then must not this someone have fulfilled the commandments of the One and Only? Where is the Wisdom of your planet?

"Your planet is great, your people are great, too, and the atmosphere of your planet is fabulous. If your world has been endowed so marvellously, then why would you need to call sages from the Earth — and not the best ones at that?

"You told us at the first reception that the Earth was renowned in the Cosmos for her Wisdom. I didn't believe it, O King and Father! For what is the Earth? Can it be that we, the wise ones, really don't know? We know this, after all! And I was immensely surprised when my friends forgot this, as they zealously set out to fulfil the duties entrusted to them, not realizing that a trap was concealed therein.

"Where was there a blessing for educating this planet? Have they forgotten that the blessing for education is given by the One and Only? Whence did they get their pride, which forced them to accept your offer?

"How can I be a teacher for children whose parents I do not even know? Pride alone could cloud their minds, but I, Thales of Argos, have not succumbed to it. You, O King and Father, said yourself that your people are good, kind, noble, and wise. We have already found the purity of morals, we have already found Wisdom — so then, why does this place need the Wisdom of the Earth here? Tell me this."

However, the King and Father, who actually understood this question of mine, Thales of Argos, was silent, for he knew that our conversations could be dangerous.

"Tell me, O King and Father," I continued, "where on your planet are the traces of the blessing of the One and Only? Why are there no Sages? Why are there no seeds of God? Why has there been no sowing? For the Reaper will come to your planet as well, provided it actually exists in the Cosmos."

I stretched out my hands and, with all the strength given to me by the Great Wisdom, I proclaimed:

"O One and Only Father, the Unknown, the Ineffable One! Send me Thy Ray, that I may overcome the temptations surrounding me! Destroy everything that has appeared before my eyes as a consequence of the human pride of pathetic little worms, O Ineffable One! Hear me!

For behold — I am the only one who, left with my Wisdom, has realized that Thou alone canst save me."

And after completing my prayer, I looked at the King and Father, and a quiet joy became resplendent in my heart. The colours of the hall faded, the King's garments faded, and his royal pride faded. He somehow became shrivelled and shrunken, and only his eyes stared pitifully at me. I understood everything and uttered the Great Formula of the Initiated. A groan reverberated, thunder rang out as though worlds were collapsing, and I flew right into the abyss; yet I did not lose consciousness. I could feel someone's marvellous, warm hands embrace me, and felt the gentle face of my Mother Isis. I heard Her voice: "O Argive, My beloved son, who has overcome human pride by Wisdom! Argive, My wonderful son! I shall Myself ignite the Fire of the Great Initiate on your brow."

Lulled by the voice of the Goddess, I fell asleep, and when I woke up, I found myself in a beautiful meadow of divine Hellas. From the forest came the Goddess Pallas Athena and said to me:

"O Argive! In my person, the Gods of Hellas greet you."

And everything around began to sing — forest, water, fauna: "Greetings to you, Thales of Argos, greetings, greetings..." — this is how my homeland welcomed me. And no matter where I went, everyone knew me, everyone greeted me. Flowers gently nodded their heads, birds trustingly alighted on my shoulder, and people were somehow marvellously affectionate. Yet I was in a hurry to see my Master. He gently met me, clasping me in his arms, and only in his eyes did I detect sadness.

"Argive," he said to me, "out of twelve, only you have returned."

We were on our way to greet the King and Father of the planet and, after a few days' journey through the desert sands, we found ourselves at his Oasis. The King and Father received me and sanctified the sign ignited on my forehead by a Holy Hand.

"O Argive," he said, "you are the only existing example. The serpent of pride can be overcome by the heart alone, but you have succeeded in defeating it with your mind: you have thereby become the first to win. However, this will serve you in that you will not remain in the bowels of humanity, for you have started to follow an uncharacteristic path."

All these great words came true in my soul — the soul of Thales of Argos. I searched but did not find it possible to enter any arena of human activity. I have always felt some kind of coldness towards humanity. Therefore, you will find the name of Thales of Argos only in secret Sanctuaries, recorded in the annals with bright letters. And on the whole planet Earth there are only three or four places with which I support communication. These are the acquaintances whom I connected with during the times of Christ the Saviour. I support them alone — all others are alien to me.

In the mind of my friend Empedocles I read the question: Who was the King and Father of this unknown planet? But he did not exist at all. He was simply a plastic dream of the magicians. It was a great test given by the Three. And do you know how much time the dream lasted? No more than three minutes, for such dreams take place in a space where there is no time. They are made not in physical space, but in psychical.

**Thales of Argos**

# III. The Proclamation of Cosmic Love

*Thales of Argos to Empedocles,*
*the son of Miles of Athens —*
*at the Supreme Wisdom of the Goddess*
*Pallas Athena — rejoice!*

L ET US REND ASUNDER the mists of the past, my
friend Empedocles, and come with me to the sphere
which you, people of the 20th century, call a fairy tale,
yet we, the never-dying consciousness of the Sons of the
Wisdom that dwells in the annals of the Universe, term
a true story.

It was night, and Selene, like a diamond ribbon, was
reflected in the mysterious waters of the Nile. I, Thales
of Argos, was standing on the tower of the temple of Isis,
recording on a roll of papyrus my calculations regarding
the ascent of a new star of Horus in the constellation of
Canis Major.

At this point a tender hand fell on my shoulder, and
I heard the soft voice of my Master, the Great Heraclitus.

"Argive!" he said to me. "Do you know the story of
the glorious Queen of Sheba, the beautiful Balqis?"

"Master! You know that for thousands of years, I have
been immersed in the study of the great manuscripts of
Existence," and I pointed to the shoreless starry sky spread
out before us. "When could I possibly explore the history
of the queens of the Earth, though they be just as beautiful as the queen of the stellar sky — the Morning Star?!"

Heraclitus silently shook his head.

"Argive!" he said. "Your response is tinged with irony,
which the mind of the son of noble Hellas cannot do
without, but, believe me, your Master, that it was not for

idle chatter that I asked you this question. Sit down, my son, and listen to me."

I sat down next to my Teacher, and his quiet, harmonious speech started to pour forth. It was so quiet and mellifluous that it sometimes completely merged with the sounds of the rays of pale Selene, who had splashed her light upon me, as well as upon my Master, the tower of the temple of Isis, the waters of the mysterious Nile, and the enigmatic depth of the mute desert which stretched beyond the river.

And here is what my Teacher narrated to me:

"When the Fire of the Earth devoured the Black Land before the birth of the blessed Atlantis, and the massifs of the pristine Lemuria became the bottom of the ocean, the catastrophe did not affect the temple of the Goddess of Life, which for a long time was an abode of the King of the Black — the mysterious Arraim. But long before the catastrophe, no one knew where the great King had disappeared to, leaving his land, his people, his temple, and his only daughter, who became the first priestess of the Goddess of Life. Surrounded by seven wise priests, she, this daughter, the beautiful Balqis, courageously faced the terrible catastrophe and came through it with fortitude.

"When at last, after many months, the clouds of ash and smoke which had obscured the vault of the sky finally scattered, and when the inhabitants of the temple of the Goddess of Life found themselves on a small island surrounded by the muddy, foamy waves of a new ocean, the beautiful Balqis performed the first act of worship before the altar of the Goddess of Life. She vowed — in a voice for all to hear — to dedicate her life to finding her father — the mysterious Arraim, for she was aware that the breath of the Goddess of Eternal Life rested upon him, and so he could not die.

"And then the oldest of the priests came forward — the most senior elder Kenan, whose third eye saw even the great perished race of the Titans of the North — and he said:

" 'Balqis! How can you make a vow without knowing whether our great Lord, the Son of Reason, Arraim, wants you to search for him? For behold — as far back as when the Titans of the North dwelt on our planet, the mysterious Arraim had already been on the Earth, which was not his cradle at all. For another Heaven and another Earth in different depths of the Cosmos had witnessed his birth. No matter how fair and wise you are, Balqis, you are still but a mere blade of grass along his enigmatic, incomprehensible path. Once the period of your life passes, the earth will claim your body, bent with age, while he, great and mysterious, will proceed further, and each of his steps will be equal to thousands of your lives...'

"Frowning her brows, the beautiful Balqis impatiently listened to the wise words of the three-eyed priest.

" 'Kenan!' she exclaimed. 'Your third eye can see far, yet it is unable to discern the depths of my heart — the heart of Arraim's daughter, the wise Balqis. Bring Arra here,' she briefly ordered the priests and turned her face towards the statue of the Goddess.

"Kenan shook his head with disapproval.

" 'Balqis, Balqis!' he said. 'Just think: what forces do you want to touch? What laws do you want to turn in your favour? After all, the abilities of Arra have so far been used only for the communication with the Lords of Life and with the Goddess Herself!'

" 'Go away, old man,' said Balqis angrily. 'Am I no longer the daughter of Arraim and the high priestess of the Goddess?'

"She straightened up — and indeed! — there was so much divinely beautiful in her wondrous figure, breathing with such unspeakable might that the old priest drooped and, muttering something, quietly stepped back.

"Meanwhile, the priests brought into the temple a marvellous girl, rather short of stature. She was of another, unknown race, for her skin was white as snow, in contrast to the dark brown skin of the Lemurians. Her eyes were not blue-emerald, like that of the beautiful Balqis, but black. Her hair did not fall in wavy curls around her shoulders, but cascaded right to the floor. And all her essence seemed to be imbued with something ethereal, not belonging to here: it was as though the breath of another world had entered together with her beneath the arches of the temple.

"The old priests were aware that it would be in vain to look for the father and mother of Arra among the Lemurians. It was known that brave seafarer Thalasael had brought back several families of these strange people from his voyage to the mysterious icy deserts of the far South. The all-wise Arraim immediately gave an order to place the women in temples and taught priests to make use of their strange, enigmatic abilities. The men of this unknown tribe soon all died out, and only the women continued to live a life within the temples — a life that can only be compared to that of hothouse flowers.

"Upon entering, the girl fearfully looked around.

" 'Come here, Arra,' Balqis told her imperiously. 'Come and sit in a sacred place.'

"The girl obediently came to the altar and sat down at its base in a kind of a chair made of basalt and encrusted with multicoloured gemstones. Balqis put on her head a hoop of gold with a polished disc with a huge diamond affixed to the front of it. She carefully turned Arra's head so that the centre of the disc could catch the reflection of the Sun from the gigantic golden concave disc that hung on a pillar in the middle of the temple.

"The pillar was movable, and the mechanism which turned it was designed so that the rays of the Sun were always focused on the centre of the disc. When the focuses of the discs coincided, Arra's eyes closed, and she immersed herself in a mysterious dream of a Second Life — a dream whose principles are known to you, Argive, as one who is Initiated.

"And here the sleeping girl started to speak:

" 'What is it you want from me, Balqis?'

" 'Find my father,' said Balqis authoritatively.

" 'I see him,' the response followed almost immediately.

" 'Ask how to find him!'

"After a brief silence, the sleeping girl replied:

" 'He says you should not search for him, as his feet are treading the path of God, which you cannot follow, Balqis. This way is not for mortals.'

"Balqis angrily furrowed her eyebrows.

" 'Tell him,' she screamed, 'that he has no right to repudiate his daughter! For on what path were his feet when he conceived me? I want to be close to him.'

" 'In no way does he repudiate you, Balqis,' Arra answered, 'for he is always with you. But even in conceiving you, he was obeying the Law of God. However, you, as a mortal, cannot be with him...'

"Balqis stared gloomily at the face of Arra.

" 'Very well,' she said with difficulty. 'Turn your eyes away from my father, Arra. Listen to me: could your marvellous spirit find its way to the Eternal Fire of the Earth's Life?'

"The priests shuddered... With a gesture of despair the ancient Kenan lowered his head. Deadly paleness engulfed the face of the sleeping girl. Almost inaudibly her lips whispered:

" 'I can... I know... I see... But if I tell you, my spark of life will fade away...'

"The beautiful Balqis impatiently shrugged her shoulders:

" 'So what? You must tell me... I then will help you to be incarnated again and be close to me...'

" 'This is not within your power, Balqis,' said the sleeping girl. I shall never be close to you... I am afraid of all who do not fulfil the Will of the One and Only...'

" 'Enough!' Balqis stamped her foot. 'I want to know and will know, even if the whole Earth crumbles because of this. Speak — I am listening!'

"A crowd of priests rushed out of the temple in Kenan's wake, unwilling to hear a terrible answer. We shall not listen to it either, Argive. It is enough for you to know that the beautiful Balqis got what she demanded, at the cost of poor Arra's life.

"She discovered the road to the Eternal Fire of the Earth's Life and actually came across this Fire, and the life of the planet was placed at her disposal. Are you not struck with amazement, Argive, at Balqis' excessive impertinence? Who knows, Argive, maybe in addition to the planetary life she also received as much in the way of extended suffering?

"Now she reigns in Sheba, to the north of the land of Hor, and she rules wisely, for she has had time to become wise. However, she never gets tired of searching for her father..."

"But we know the Four-time-Greatest One, Master," said I, Thales of Argos.

"He wished to reveal himself to us," Heraclitus replied to me, "but he will never reveal himself to his disobedient daughter. Now, every thousand years, she organizes a great Festival of Wisdom and assembles representatives of all Initiations — the great sages of the world — in the vain hope of learning from them her father's secret. Yet even here there is slyness, Argive, for many of the wise ones trade faithfulness to the sign of their Initiation for loyalty to the most beautiful woman on the planet and forever remain chained to her wondrous throne."

"But this is a fall, isn't it, my Master?" I asked.

"Yes," Heraclitus replied in grief. "But the beautiful Balqis immediately endows the fallen ones with the Fire of the Earth's Life and thereby prevents their death. Yet anyway, the mighty Arraim instantly extinguishes the memory of himself in those who knew him...

"The Theban Sanctuary," Heraclitus added after a pause, "has lost three of its sons at her throne..."

"Then why does the Sanctuary send its Initiates there, to this festival?" asked I, Thales of Argos.

"But what Sanctuary has the right to decline a test?" the Wise One answered me with a question. "Now the time of festival is approaching, and the beautiful Balqis has already sent us her invitation..."

"So you decided to send me, Master!" calmly added I, Thales of Argos.

"Yes, my son," the Wise One said to me. "Only your soul, O son of Hellas, has a tranquillity like that of basalt rocks in the depths of the ocean, and our Sanctuary does not worry about you..."

"Let it be!" I replied, for then I was able to obey.

In a boat along the sacred waters of the Nile, I reached the mountains of Ethiopia, safely passing by the encampment of the wild sons of the desert and the Valley of the

Dead. After letting go in peace the Phœnician sailors who accompanied me, I entered a crevasse in the mountains, forcing a wise Serpent crawling ahead to point out the way for me.

It was not the custom of the Theban Sanctuary to travel in luxury, for we knew that the splendour and magnificence of the Earth were mere dust under the heel of the Lord, and our Wisdom was madness in His eyes. Lonely and destitute, the wise sons of the Beacon of Eternity were walking upon the face of the planet, yet there was no one richer than we.

Two days later, on the way I encountered a magnificent caravan, which consisted of three dozen camels and a dozen elephants, accompanied by a whole detachment of swarthy, luxuriously dressed horsemen in gold helmets: three of the elephants were white and bore on their strong backs whole towers of gold, silver, platinum, and precious stones, draped in fine silk fabrics of the Dravidian Country. These were the Sons of the Triangle that followed the Festival of Wisdom.

I humbly stepped aside and, through will-power, temporarily extinguished the sign of the Beacon of Eternity invisibly shining on my forehead, lest the Sons of the Triangle recognized me.

And after it followed another caravan of white camels, but at the head of the caravan was the wise Initiate of the Lunar Sanctuary — a grey-haired, strong Chaldean — who sat in a sedan-chair made of ivory, decorated with rows of rubies and a fringe of fine golden lace. The sedan-chair was carried by twelve black slaves from the land of the Distant Cape, which I, Thales of Argos, once visited when the Sanctuary of Thebes sent me to accompany the brave Phœnician Hanno on his distant voyage.

At first the gaze of the wise Chaldean slid indifferently over me. But, after stopping at the head of the Serpent that had lain down at my feet, his gaze blazed up with the fire of understanding, and a derisive yet good-natured smile came over his lips. He made a sign, and the slaves stopped.

"O wise foreigner!" the Chaldean addressed me tenderly. "I apologize for my brothers in Wisdom from the Symbol of the Triangle who did not recognize you. But their Wisdom is so great that in its immensity, it cannot fit into the sinful Earth, and therefore their gaze is always directed upwards — to Heaven. On the other hand, the gaze of the poor old Chaldean always slides along the ground, endeavouring to pick up the grains of Wisdom they spilled. And so I have noticed the head of your quite unusual 'companion,' O wise Hellene of the Great Sanctuary of Thebes. Would you be so kind to honour my old age with your consent to share my loneliness on my next journey?"

I saw that I could not escape from the crafty wisdom of the Chaldean. There being no reason to decline the invitation, I sat down in the sedan-chair, gently releasing my guide.

"But how did you learn, O venerable Chaldean," I asked, "that I am actually a Hellene?"

"Not only a Hellene," the Chaldean smiled with cunning, "but also a descendant of the royal Atlanteans. Have you ever looked at your reflection in polished copper? Your height, your shoulders and divine physique immediately identify you as a son of the noble Hellas. And the strict calmness of your proper visage and the beauty of its lines take me back into the long distant past, when I, an old Chaldean, had the pleasure of seeing the collegium of priests of the temple of the Eternally Young

Virgin-Mother in Poseidonis. Is it not from your environment that the Divine Zoroaster came, whom I once welcomed when he wished to honour my native Chaldean city of Ur with his presence?

"As to the fact that I immediately recognized in you a pupil of the Theban Sanctuary, it was your 'companion' that suggested this to me, O noble Thales of Argos, for only the Land of Kemet has preserved relations with the Kingdom of Serpents. Yet I see that you, O Sage, want to ask me how I know your name? But was it not you who completed a renowned voyage with Hanno the Phœnician, and even visited the tribe of Cabeiri near the Pillars of Hercules? After all, this tribe is under our protection, O Sage. How could we not know you, not to mention the fact that the all-wise Heraclitus could send only you, Argive, to the festival of Queen Balqis!"

"You, the Chaldeans," I, Thales of Argos, responded to him, "refused to communicate with the Kingdom of Serpents, yet you have imbibed their Wisdom..."

"Yes, yes, Argive," said the Chaldean sadly, stroking his long beard, "but on the other hand we with our Wisdom are crawling on our bellies on the face of Mother Earth..."

I, Thales of Argos, harnessed my will and immediately transferred myself to the sphere of symbols and original sounds. After learning what I needed to learn, I came back in an instant.

"I am glad," I said quietly, "that Hermes the Thrice-Greatest, in his tireless care for his children, has afforded me the chance to have an instructive conversation with the wise Rabbi Israel from Ur of the Chaldees..."

The Chaldean looked at me intently and bowed his head with respect.

"What does the wisdom of the creeping Serpent mean compared with the wisdom of the Eagle soaring beneath the clouds, from whose sight nothing can hide," he added thoughtfully.

After several hours of travelling, spent in conversation with the wise Chaldean, we reached the garden belt surrounding the city of the Queen. Here I bade farewell to the Chaldean.

"For," I told him, "it does not befit an Initiate of Thebes to arrive on a visit to the Queen in someone else's chariot."

I, Thales of Argos, did not go into the city, but after passing around it, went into the woods, where I spent the night, devoting the hours of darkness to the conversations and evocations of spirits of Nature that I needed.

The next morning, the wonderful, fabulous gardens of Queen Balqis, enclosed by pink marble walls and irrigated by hundreds of fountains, were filled with invited guests.

There were swarthy handsome Dravidians with fixed eyes, as if blinded by the constant contemplation of Wisdom. There were the copper-red descendants of the Tlavatli from the country that had emerged from the sea to the west of wondrous Atlantis. There were black descendants of Lemuria from the bowels of Africa. There were members of the cross-eyed tribe with large feminine braids, the Atlanteans of the seventh sub-race of Mongoloids, who lived in the mysterious walled country on the shores of the Great Lemurian Sea. There were white magicians from the land of northern ice-deserts. Also there were the long-bearded, crafty-wise Chaldeans.

There is no way to describe the magnificence and splendour of their caravans, as well as of the clothes they wore, for what is there on the planet which the Wisdom of earthly magic is unable to find or do?

However, the richest and most spectacular were the vestures worn by Queen Balqis' entourage of sages surrounding her fabulous throne, in addition to a few lions, one of which obediently placed his majestic head under the feet of the Empress.

Do I really need to tell you, Empedocles, about Balqis' beauty? Rarely had heroes of Hellas ever dreamt of such charm, and the beautiful Helen herself would have looked like a most ordinary woman in comparison to her. Her marvellous beauty seemed to be supported from within by the brilliance of great Wisdom, great pride crowned her forehead with a royal halo, and mighty Will gleamed with sparkles in her eyes, blue as the noonday sky.

Eagerly Balqis questioned the guests who came to her, skilfully directing the conversation to topics of her own interest. But so far, apparently, she couldn't find out anything, for a wrinkle of hidden vexation had furrowed her marble brow.

"O wise ones!" rang out her enchanting voice. "As always, I want to start our festival with serving the God of the Sun, yet still there is no Initiate of Thebes to whom belongs the first place in this service. Perhaps, he is late, or," a scoff could be heard in her voice, "the wise Heraclitus is afraid of losing yet another son, for behold — three Theban Initiates now comprise the embellishment of my throne..."

"O wise Queen, may the blessing of Adonai rest upon you," the insinuating voice of Rabbi Israel was heard to say, "the Theban Initiate will come, for I met him yesterday on the way to your marvellous city... This is a wise Hellene, Thales of Argos..."

"A Hellene? So much the better," the Queen smiled. "My first three guests were Egyptians... I love the noble sons of Hellas."

And here the ranks of the invited quietly parted, and under Queen Balqis' large feathery fans I appeared — I, Thales of Argos, bearer of the Beacon of Eternity, a descendant of the royal dynasty of Atlantis.

There were no adornments of the Earth on me, for I had my Wisdom with me. I was clothed only with a white woollen chiton, the body of the Living Belt girdling me, for behold — the Queen of Serpents herself had embraced my waist with her powerful ring; her head was against my chest, as she proudly and menacingly looked around with her blood-ruby eyes. A simple willow staff was in my hands.

"The all-wise Great Heraclitus, the servant of the Eternal Symbol of Life, sends you greetings, O Queen," I said quietly. "And I, Thales of Argos, wish you to rejoice, O beautiful Balqis, in the Supreme Wisdom of the Great Goddess Pallas Athena..."

Immediately around me a wide empty space formed, for never before had the Queen of Serpents appeared like this among people, even initiated ones. Her small head, crowned with a diadem made from a strange lunar stone, rested on my shoulder.

The wise Queen Balqis herself turned pale after looking into the eyes of the regal Serpent.

"Greetings to you, wise messenger of Thebes," said Balqis, her voice trembling. "I swear upon the great memory of my father," she exclaimed: "Never have I, the Queen of Sheba, the Lady of the Earth's Fire, beheld the arrival of such a Sage!

"There are no words," she went on, "to express my gratitude to Heraclitus for sending you, the wisest of mortals, to me, for whoever heard — or when — that the Regal Empress of Serpents agreed to obey a human being? Tell me, wise Argive, how you achieved this? Or is it a new secret of the Wisdom of the Theban Sanctuary?"

"It is no secret, Queen," I replied calmly. "I have attained this by something you do not have!"

Balqis glanced into my eyes with surprise:

"Something I do not have? But what is it I do not have, Argive?"

"The Seed of Cosmic Love, O beautiful and wise Balqis," I said.

Whispers were heard in the crowd of the Initiated, who all moved towards me, seemingly involuntarily.

"Cosmic Love?" the Queen asked again, furrowing her eyebrows. "What is this Cosmic Love? Oh, I know it, Argive," she smiled cunningly. "At least ask these three," — and here she pointed out to me three tall, gloomy figures standing behind her throne. "They are your brothers by the Sanctuary. Argive, ask them if the beautiful Balqis understands what love is?"

Calmly and clearly I, Thales of Argos, looked into the shining eyes of the Queen.

"I am not talking about that kind of love, O Balqis," was my answer. "I am talking about the Love for all that exists, that lives and breathes and on which the Divine Ra pours His light and warmth..."

"For all that exists?" asked Balqis. "So then I must love both a snake and my black slave?"

And the pearly laughter of the Queen rippled across the hall, and was caught by her retinue. However, the Initiates did not laugh, for their Wisdom had sensed a new Revelation in my words.

"Indeed, both the snake and your black slave, O Queen," I confirmed calmly, "for the snake is your sister and the slave is your brother."

Anger momentarily flared up in Balqis' eyes, though it was immediately extinguished.

"What is this new teaching that you are proclaiming, Argive?" she asked with restraint, biting her lip.

"This is not a new teaching, O Balqis," I replied. "When a father gives his son a spear for the first time, it seems new to the lad, even though it may have already struck many. At present, the Three Sages said," — and here I raised my voice, which roared like thunder under the arches of the hall — "that it is time to proclaim to humanity about the Seed of Cosmic Love... I say the *Seed*, O Queen, for the very embodiment of Love will be brought to the Earth by the Greatest One, whose Name is a Cosmic Mystery, and the time of His Coming is known only to the One and Only."

Furrowing her eyebrows, Balqis embraced the entire assembly with her fiery gaze.

"Has anyone among the Sages heard of this teaching about the Seed of Love that the Theban alien proclaims?" she asked loudly.

A tall old man with a grey moustache and plait quietly stepped forward from the crowd. Under his thick eyebrows, what appeared to be two round, absolutely transparent discs were rather strangely attached; through them, strictly and calmly, gazed the eyes of inexplicable wisdom.

"I am an ambassador of the Land of the Dragon from the shores of the Great Lemurian Sea," he said. "My name is Lao-Tzu, I am a servant of the One God, the Perfect Dao — the Dao in which all things are hidden and united: including the wise Theban messenger, as well as you, most beautiful Queen, and the Serpent, and the black slave, along with me, a humble servant of the Dao. And this great mystery of the unity of all-in-all is resolved only through Divine Love, which the wise Hellene has proclaimed to us...

"Let the cover of the Dao be above your head, Argive," he addressed me, "for I have heard the Great Proclamation of yours and now I shall quietly enter my cave to venerate the land of my ancestors, for I feel that, when the Greatest of the Great Ones comes, He will call upon my shadow, and the humble prophet of the Perfect Dao will arrive to serve Him..."

And in this elder there was so much marvellous simplicity and wise peace that I, Thales of Argos, bowed before him, and the Queen of Serpents began to hiss amiably, shaking her emerald head over my shoulders.

Silence fell in the hall.

"And who are those Three you were talking about, Hellene?" the now pale-looking Balqis asked me.

"You know one of them, O Queen," I replied calmly, "that was the Four-time-Greatest Arraim, the priest of the Morning Star, the Father and Ruler of the Black..."

Balqis' hands convulsively grasped hold of the armrests of her throne, and she impetuously leaned forward.

"Father!" she exclaimed, her voice almost choking, "do you know him, have you seen him, my Sage?"

"I know him and have seen him, O Balqis," I said.

"When and where?"

"Yesterday, in the forest near your city, O Queen," was my answer.

The eyes of the beautiful Queen blazed up with wild fire.

"Here... near..." she repeated. "And did he not order you to tell me something?"

"That he did, O Queen," said I, Thales of Argos. "He told me to tell you that your searches and efforts to see him are futile, even if you stole the Fire not only of one planet but of all nine. You will never see him, for you have violated the laws of the temple of the Goddess of Life by daring to penetrate to the Fire of the Earth and thereby enter into relations with the forces of Chaos. In so doing, you did not spare the precious life of the prophetess, the servant of the Goddess. The beauty and wisdom bestowed upon you, you have employed to plunge wise Initiates into the abyss of falling. So, here, O Balqis, is the last commandment of your father's: you will see him only when you transform the Fire of the Earth burning within you into the flame of Cosmic Love, and then the Greatest of the Greatest, Who is to come into the world, will unite you with your father..."

Cold and menacing, the beautiful Balqis rose from the throne, her blue eyes blazing with the gloomy fire of anger.

"Come to me, Sages of my Kingdom!" her voice resounded. "Your Queen, your Lady has been offended by an unknown stranger. He is a liar. My father could not use such degrading words in speaking to me. Let the Lord of the Earth's Fire rise and incinerate my enemies!"

And surrounded by the traitors of secret Sanctuaries, she, enveloped in a cloud of crimson light, started to sing a wild song of invocation, in which her servants echoed her. The assembly shuddered: I watched as the newly-come Initiates left the hall one by one. And finally there remained only I, Thales of Argos, the wise elder Lao-Tzu who kept looking at the Queen with sad interest, and

Rabbi Israel, who had covered his head with a cloak, muttering something under his breath.

The front wall of the hall had already collapsed and in its place a new wall arose out of the dark haze, rising in clumps from some kind of abyss. I could already feel the approach of the Earth's Fire, chilling and dreadful. And now slowly, but slowly, the Queen of Serpents crept down from me and started to whirl in a rhythmic dance near the throne of Balqis, as though tracing a magic circle around the three of us. The Serpent's head, burning with blue light, was constantly directed towards the wall of gloom, while her ruby eyes were like arrows piercing the vapours of the planet's bowels.

But I, Thales of Argos, was calm, for great was the power of my soul. And I watched as next to Rabbi Israel emerged the outlines of two spirits of the Moon with horned tiaras on their heads, while the spirits of the desert were swarming in a thick crowd behind the wise Atlantean Lao-Tzu's back.

And in the gloom of fog someone's gigantic crimson-red face was now rising. We could see their attentive and angry eyes, and a body seemingly covered with tongues of flame was appearing. That was Baphomet himself, the Lord of the Underworld, the King of Tartarus, the Great Rejected One.

For a minute or two, his spiteful eyes rested upon us, and then slowly turned towards Balqis, who was reaching out her arms to him.

"Mad Balqis!" his voice reverberated like a distant roar of the fiery surf in a volcano crater. "Why have you called me? How can I fight with myself, when the Queen of Serpents has risen against you?

"Mad Balqis! I am the Lord of the Earthly Fire, but here the spirits of the Moon have been up in arms against me, and I am powerless against them.

"Mad Balqis! What can I do with the Hellene who is out of your favour, when the blessing of your father, Arraim, rests upon him? And do not the spirits of the desert — the servants of the One whose name is Silence — stand behind the third?

"Mad Balqis! This is your punishment, for what is common among you, my servant, and your father Arraim whose feet are on the path of the One Whose name I cannot pronounce? Deal with this on your own as you see fit, but remember that no Cosmic Love can ever pluck you out of my hands and heart!"

"You are the spirit of falsehood and denial!" I, Thales of Argos, dauntlessly thundered in response to the last words of the Rejected Spirit. "Let the Queen of Serpents, the spirits of the Moon, and the spirits of the desert leave. Let I, Thales of Argos, remain alone, the bearer of the Sacred Beacon of Eternity with the Seed of Cosmic Love in my heart. And let us join a terrible and formidable battle for the soul of the beautiful Balqis, as her father, Arraim the Four-time-Greatest, has entrusted to me not to destroy her, but to put her on the path of good!"

The Rejected Spirit looked at me in great surprise. And then his brow seemed to smooth out, his eyes extinguished their anger and began to shine with some strange other-worldly, almost compassionate light.

"Brave Hellene," his scoffing voice sounded forth. "Or do you really think that the predestination of my being consists in the fight against all sorts of human worms who imagine themselves to be sages only because the sign of the cross burns on their foreheads? Or has not the all-wise Heraclitus revealed to you that any combat with me is a struggle in time? Do you have enough Manvantaras at your disposal, O Theban worm, to take on this fight? Go your way, worm — and who knows? Over time, if you grow wiser, perhaps we shall talk with you. After all, among all human worms, you have the most promising future..."

At once the fire of his eyes faded away, the outlines of his head and body crumbled, the chaotic fog dispersed, and again the wall of the hall emerged from it.

I looked around. Peacefully rocking back and forth, Rabbi Israel was still praying with his head covered. The wise Lao-Tzu was standing thoughtfully stroking his beard. And further, near Queen Balqis' throne, the huddling crowd of her sages were lying in the most unnatural positions. Balqis herself, pale as death, was sitting motionless on her throne, staring into the ruby eyes of the Queen of Serpents, who with a hiss continued her mysterious dance in front of her.

I uttered a spell, and she slowly came back to me and crawled on me again, girdling my body.

Balqis' sages once more began to show signs of life, while the Queen herself, after letting out a deep sigh, covered her face with her hands.

The silence lasted for a long time. Finally, the Queen said in a stammering voice:

"You have defeated the beautiful Balqis, Argive. Go and proclaim her loss to the world..."

"You are truly mad, O Balqis," I replied. "I have defeated no one — it was your father who triumphed — Arraim the Four-time-Greatest — along with Divine Love. Yet if you admit defeat, then I ask of you: Set free at once those three Initiates of the Theban Sanctuary whom you have chained to your throne by your beauty and wisdom."

The beautiful Balqis shrugged her shoulders.

"Why do I need them, Argive!" she said. "Take them. But do tell me, O wise Hellene, did you stand up for my soul before the Lord of the Earth's Fire on your behalf or that of my father?"

"On my behalf, O Queen," I replied.

"For I know that Cosmic Love reigns supreme in the heart of Arraim: and so how could he abandon his child to the death of Pralaya? And what can oppose the wisdom and power of the First Magician of the planet?"

"You are truly wise, Hellene," said Balqis in a weak voice upon reflection. "And now, depart from me, my Sages," she addressed the three of us, "and leave poor Balqis alone so that I can think of... Cosmic Love," she concluded with a slight sneer.

"May the Dao be with you, O lost soul," Lao-Tzu gently replied to her.

"Let Adonai, blessed be His Name, sow peace in your distraught soul," Rabbi Israel quietly uttered.

"Let Divine Love illumine your heart, Balqis, and may you return to fatherly embraces!" I said in a loud voice — I, Thales of Argos — and threw upon the Queen the veil from the breathing of my Wisdom.

Immediately her cheeks flushed and her blues eyes became ignited with life and power.

"I shall not forget your wishes, Argive," she said in a ringing voice. "Three times I had defeated the Theban Sanctuary, but on the fourth, you took your full revenge with interest, O wise Hellene. However, Heaven is my witness that I harbour no anger towards you in my heart."

And so we left the beautiful Balqis. This time I, Thales of Argos, took four camels from Rabbi Israel, putting on three of them the traitors of the Sanctuary that I had won back.

Warmly, with mutual blessings, the three of us bade farewell, not forgetting to give our breath to the wise Queen of Serpents as a reward.

And the wise Lao-Tzu said to me upon parting:

"Argive! There are many hours, days, and years in the infinite Dao, but the happiest of them will be that one on which I shall meet with you again, my noble Hellene. My soul has read in the book of Dao that I shall be called upon by the Greatest of the Greatest to serve Him. Remember, Argive, if I forget at that time about our meeting, you will remind me of it!"

"I also know that it is not the last time I am to meet you, Sages," confirmed Rabbi Israel. "Truly, our planet is too small for the Wise Ones..."

Great was the celebration in the Theban Sanctuary when I, Thales of Argos, arrived there.

With marvellous magnificence, we held a divine service at the temple of Isis, and here, the Thrice-Greatest Hermes himself appeared to us in a fiery cloud and crowned me, Thales of Argos, with the Ray of the Highest Initiation. And then the Hierophant of the Sanctuary, the wise Heraclitus, brought the Fire of Space down on the heads of the traitors whom I delivered, giving their souls to the power of the Queen of Serpents, who had so faithfully served me in my journey.

Peace be upon your head, Empedocles! In my further stories you will meet again all the persons I named in my narrative.

**Thales of Argos**

# IV. In the Garden of Magdala

*Thales of Argos to Empedocles,*
*the son of Miles of Athens —*
*at the Supreme Wisdom*
*of the Great Galilean*
*Teacher — rejoice!*

LISTEN, MY FRIEND, attentively, for never has a more strange and mysterious true story troubled the ear of a mortal. Indeed, a true story, I, Thales of Argos, say, — no legend!

When the Beacon of Eternity crowned with its bright ray my brow as a sign of the highest Initiation of the Theban Sanctuary, I, Thales of Argos, and Clodius of Macedonia (who was honoured with the same degree), accepted from the hands of the Great Hierophant a drink from the Cup of Life, and he sent us into a secret Abode, to the Son of Wisdom — Heraclitus, whom human hearsay named the Obscure, for people understood neither him nor his Teaching.

How many years passed while we were absorbing his Wisdom, how many times we left our Abode to bring certain little crumbs of knowledge to people, and returned again — there is no need to count.

In one of such incarnations, when I was in the world under the personality of a Stoic philosopher, I found you, my friend Empedocles, near the wise Socrates, and strengthened those threads which have bound us from the times of the City of the Golden Gates, now resting under the waves of the ocean.

One day our wise Master called us to him and said:

"Go into the world to greet on my behalf our New Teacher, as He comes into the world. I cannot tell you where you will find Him. Let your own Wisdom be your guiding finger..."

"But if this Teacher is so great," said Clodius of Macedonia, "then why do not you, O Sage, yourself go out to welcome Him?"

"This is because," Heraclitus answered us, "I know who He is. And here my knowledge tells me that I am unworthy of meeting Him. But you do not know Him — you only know from me that He is a Great Teacher, and nothing more. Only the blind are able to look at the Sun with impunity..."

At that time I was still able to obey and silently left with Clodius. The next day camels were carrying us to the North, to the Sanctuary of the black-faced Ishtar. There, the last black priests, silent like stones of the desert, directed us to the Great Centre, to the One whose name is Silence, whose count of years has been lost by the planetary calendar and whose destiny is to wait for the end, so as to be the last Grave-digger of the Earth. When Clodius and I prostrated ourselves before him in the dust, he gently lifted us up and said:

"Children! I saw Him when He was an infant. I bowed to Him. If my son Heraclitus sent you to Him, then go. Now He is already sowing the seed. But remember, children, once you find Him, you will lose everything..."

The Son of the Morning Star, whose name is Silence, had nothing else to tell us. His existence is a mystery, and he is to be the Godfather and the Grave-digger of the Earth, whose title is Priest of the Ineffable One.

He said nothing, but his hand pointed out the North for us. Again we got lost in the desert. We did not say a word, just catching the magnetic currents of Wisdom so familiar to us. We were unafraid of "losing everything," for we were able to obey...

And now we reached Palestine, from where, it seemed to us, the currents of Wisdom were emanating, so strangely mixed with the disgusting fluids of a people — the servants of the Lunar power. We were choking in the dense atmosphere of temples, wherein false wisdom, hypocrisy, and cruelty reigned. We talked with priests — cunning, rich people; we enquired of them whether they had Wise Teachers among them. It happened that a few were pointed out to us; yet, alas, we found people stupider and more false than the crowd, and even crueller.

The people — the common people, oppressed and fooled by the priests — were willing to share with us their legends, which were full of superstitions and distortions. But I, Thales of Argos, and Clodius of Macedonia heard there the echoes of the great legends of the Red Race, refracted through the scientific prisms of solar Chaldea and mangled by the wild ignorance of Judaic priests — a miserable heritage of the renegade and madman Osarseph. This people was waiting for a Teacher — but a Teacher in purple and bronze, who was obliged, in its opinion, to yield the world to the supremacy of greedy priests. It knew nothing about the Teacher who had already come.

But then one day we heard this speech from a noble Judean, who was born and lived most of his life in Athens:

"I, Nicodemus, can show you, O philosophers, one strange man. He lives in a cave on the banks of the Jordan River. Go to him and ask him any necessary questions. He is naked and destitute, and his disciples are unsociable and savage in appearance. His name is John. Go quickly, because I have heard a rumour that an order has been given to take him into custody in view of his incessant attacks on priests and even on the king himself. However, O philosophers," Nicodemus added with a smile, "you will hardly find in him what you need... But why will not you, Sages, meet with one whom our people call a prophet?"

And we saw that John. He was truly a terrible sight to behold: devoid of attire, a thin, emaciated, hairy body, black nails; the locks of his long, never-combed hair and beard tumbling down on his shoulders and chest; his voice hoarse and clamorous. We saw him sitting on a rock on the river bank in front of a crowd of kneeling people. He was swinging his arms and, furiously, foaming at the mouth, spewing curses and swearings. He was calling the wrath of God down on the human herd — miserable, dirty, and hungry as they were — and he threatened them with terrible tortures. Obediently and slavishly, the people listened to him...

However, we, on whose brows was burning the Beacon of Eternity, saw his fiery eyes and recognized in them the sacred fire of the Son of Life. We saw his fluidic emanations, in which there was nothing similar to the fluids of a human being... And I, Thales of Argos, and Clodius of Macedonia drooped our heads in reflection on the paths unknown to us, along which the Perfect One was sending His currents into the world of matter, for here, before us, under this most filthy appearance, was undoubtedly the Son of Life, and not a human being.

"We have come closer, Argive," Clodius said to me. "Is this really the purpose of our wanderings?"

But I, Thales of Argos, was cooler and calmer than Clodius, and my not-so-hot and quick mind was more earthly and therefore — alas! — wiser.

"Only a human being can be a Teacher, Clodius," I replied. "And this is the Son of Life!"

We waited until the one called John plunged the whole crowd into the waters of the Jordan, whereupon the whole crowd — cursed, its wet body covered with spittle but happy in spirit — proceeded towards the city with a howl — some kind of raucous chant.

We calmly approached the prophet, who had been left alone on the shore of the shallow and muddy river. I, Thales of Argos, raised my hand and poured over John's head and back currents of warm greetings from the Sanctuary and, in a secret language of Sacred Wisdom, uttered a formula calling upon the Sons of Life.

John slowly turned to face us. His eyes, which a minute earlier had appeared so menacing, were now shining with indescribable kindness.

"What do the sons of earthly Wisdom need from a servant of the Lord?" sounded a quiet and harmonious voice, which just a short while ago was roaring furiously and frightfully with curses and swearings.

"We are looking for the Great Teacher," answered I, Thales of Argos. "We have brought Him greetings from the Sanctuary and Abode. Where can we find Him?"

John, the Son of Life in a human form, looked at us meekly and lovingly.

"And do you know," he asked, "what you will lose when you see Him?"

"Yes," we replied. "But we are simply obedient disciples of the Sanctuary. But then, does water cry when it evaporates in the Sun's rays, rising upwards even as it loses its water qualities?"

John smiled tenderly.

"Truly, you are wise, O noble Greeks," he replied. "How can you find the Teacher? Go to Galilee. Let the Omnibenevolent bless you with meeting Jesus of Nazareth..."

And after returning our peace to us, he went away.

And I, Thales of Argos, said to Clodius of Macedonia:

"Restrain the flight of your mind, my Macedonian friend! For behold — if the Son of Life takes on the dirty and disgusting appearance of a Judean prophet, then in what form should the Teacher manifest Himself? Do not look at the stars, look at the ground, for it is in the earthly dust that Truth is to reveal itself..."

And so, late in the evening, we arrived in a simple manner, for everything in the world of the Most High is simple.

It was evening, and there was a full moon. We were told:

"Jesus of Nazareth, whom you are seeking, has gone to the house of Lazarus, whom He resurrected from a deadly sleep. Here is the house..."

The house was surrounded by a leafy garden. When we entered the garden, two men blocked our way: one in his prime of masculine power — rude and gloomy; the other was a young man, gentle, with long flaxen hair flowing over his shoulders.

"What do you want, foreigners?" the first one asked coarsely.

"To see the Great Teacher," answered Clodius of Macedonia.

"The Teacher has not come for you Gentiles," the Judean said angrily. "You are unworthy to see Him... Go away..."

"I see that you, noble man, are a holy and righteous person," I, Thales of Argos, replied. "What can the Teacher possibly give you, if you are already holy and righteous as you are? But we Gentiles are poor and ignorant sinners, we want to learn from the Teacher... At least so that we might become as holy and righteous as you, O great and virtuous man."

Then the younger man quickly tugged at the sleeve of the chiton of the bewildered Judean, who was staring at me angrily. He whispered something to him and then, smiling tenderly, said to me:

"O noble foreigner, do not waste the arrows of your Attic wit on humiliating this poor Judean. Sit down on the bench — I shall send you one of our friends, and you can tell him everything you need."

Tired, we sat down on the bench. Yet a great fire was burning in the heart of Clodius of Macedonia and a marvellous light was flooding my own mind: we knew we had found the Teacher, for how could the Light of Eternity pouring over the humble olive garden in Magdala be hidden from the gaze of an Initiate?

And then a man appeared before us, in clean white clothes, with the seal of wisdom upon his brow. On his forehead was burning the secret sign of Initiation of the Red Race, whose Sanctuaries were hid by distant Asia. It was from Asia that the Thrice-Greatest One had come to us. It is from there where Sages had populated entire cities, and it was there where the dominion of the Triangle had been established. And when we saw that our signs of the Beacon of Eternity were no secret for him, he bowed to us and said:

"Greetings to you, brethren from Thebes. I am Thomas, a humble disciple of the One Whom you are seeking. Tell me the purpose of your journey. Who sent you?"

And our conversation poured forth, conducted in the secret language of the Sanctuary of the World. In the space of a mere hour, we learnt from Brother Thomas everything that led up to the appearance of the Teacher, and in what form He desired to be revealed to the world... We were overwhelmed by great, reverential bewilderment:

for, being accustomed to look for the small in the great, how could we grasp the great in the small?

"Truly," Clodius Macedonia exclaimed with fervour, "this Teacher has absorbed all the legends and myths of the world!"

"And transformed them into Truth," I, Thales of Argos, added. "Or have you, Clodius, forgotten what the Great Heraclitus told us? Or have you forgotten how the Priest of the Ineffable One, whose name is Silence, told us about his adoration of the Teacher at His birth? Prepare to see the embodiment of Truth, my Macedonian friend..."

Thomas stood up and bowed to me, Thales of Argos:

"I no longer have anything to tell you, my brethren," he uttered. "Your Wisdom truly serves you as a guiding light... I shall go and let the Teacher know."

As soon as he left, I, Thales of Argos, after summoning the secret name of the Ineffable One, immersed myself in contemplation of the future. And I was allowed to see something which lay at the basis of everything that time had brought me.

When I opened my eyes, in front of us was standing a woman, still young and beautiful, and with the seal of the Great Care upon her face.

"The Teacher invites you, foreigners," she quietly said.

We followed her. Clodius of Macedonia was hurrying, unable to restrain the outburst of his fiery heart, but I, Thales of Argos, was proceeding calmly, for my mind was full of the Cold of the Great Cognition, imparted to me during my brief contemplation of the future. I was bearing the cold of the whole world within me — so where could I possibly find warmth?

Thus we came to the terrace, illumined by the Moon. In a corner thereof, in the semi-darkness of an olive tree,

He was sitting — the Teacher. Here is what I, Thales of Argos, saw.

He was of high stature, rather lean. He was dressed in a simple chiton with a dusty hem. His bare feet rested on an ordinary mat of reeds. His dark brown hair and beard were neatly combed. His face was thin and appeared to be exhausted by the Great Suffering of the World. And in His eyes, I, Thales of Argos, saw all the Love of the Universe. And I understood everything, regardless of what the spiritual circle of the Teacher revealed to me, as an Initiate.

Meanwhile, Clodius of Macedonia was already lying at the feet of the Master and kissing them, irrigating the garden and terrace with his tears. The Teacher's hand was tenderly resting upon his head. The woman who brought us kept staring at me in either a semi-frightened or semi-indignant manner, for here was I, Thales of Argos, calmly standing right in front of the face of her Master.

His gaze of incarnate Love embraced me with a peaceful, heavenly caress. And His voice, like the voice of the mothers of the whole world, said to me:

"Sit down next to Me, wise Argive. Tell Me why you were looking for Me? I do not ask this of your friend... His sobbing tells Me everything. And you?"

And I, Thales of Argos, sat down at the right hand of God, for the cold of the entire world was in my mind.

"I have come to Thee, O Ineffable One," I answered calmly, "and brought Thee greetings from my Master Heraclitus. I have brought Thee greetings from the One whose name is Silence. I have brought Thee greetings from the Sanctuary and Abode. I have come to Thee so as to lose everything, for I bear within myself the Cold of the Great Cognition..."

"Then why is your friend, who has lost everything, now carrying within himself the Warmth of Great Love?" He asked me quietly.

"He has not seen what I saw, O Ineffable One," I replied calmly.

"And you, wise Argive, have you recognized Me, if you address Me thus?"

"It is impossible to recognize Thee," I replied. "It is possible to recognize only what Thou pleasest to reveal to us. And then I do not ask Thee for anything, for I have lost everything and I do not want to have anything."

Slowly and quietly His tender hand touched my head. Yet the Cold of the Great Prescience still reigned supreme in my heart and I, Thales of Argos, remained seated calmly.

"Mary," His voice resounded. "Let the flower of Divine Love, which has blossomed within your heart, tell you: which of these two pilgrims loves and knows Me more?"

The woman's eyes blazed up.

"O Master!" she said in a barely audible voice. "This one loves more," she pointed to Clodius, "but this... this one... I'm scared, Master!"

"Even Divine Love herself was frightened by your Great Suffering, Argive," He told me. "Blessed are you, Argive, for that your heart is full of courage and thereby was able to endure the Cold of the Great Cognition, also known as the Great Suffering..."

"O Teacher!" the woman interrupted Him passionately. "But this one... this one whom Thou callest Argive, he is closer to Thee!"

A smile touched the lips of the Nazarene.

"You are right, Mary," He confirmed. "Argive is closer to Me, for he has already foreseen in his heart what I am soon to endure. But he is just a human being... So, Clodius," He turned to the Macedonian, "will you follow Me?"

"I am Thine, O Master," said Clodius, sobbing.

"I am taking you to Me..."

And the hand of the Ineffable One imperiously extinguished the Beacon of Eternity burning on Clodius of Macedonia's brow.

"I have removed the cross from your forehead and now lay it upon your shoulders. You will go and will bear My yoke and My Word to countries unknown to you. People will neither know nor remember you; I am replacing your Wisdom with Love. At the end of your life, the cross which I am now laying upon you, will be your deathbed, yet you will conquer death and will come to Me.

"Henceforth I am separating you from your friend — your paths will part. And you, Argive," the Ineffable One addressed me, "you, too, have lost everything... What shall I give you in return?"

"I saw Thee and spoke with Thee," I answered calmly. "What else canst Thou give me?"

The gaze of the Ineffable One rested upon me with His great love.

"The earthly Wisdom within you is truly sanctified, Argive," He said. "Will you follow Me as well?"

"I cannot *but* follow Thee," I answered. "However, I can never follow those who follow Thee..."

"So be it," said the Nazarene sadly. "Go, Argive. I shall not remove the Beacon of Eternity from your brow. I am only returning to you the period of your human life. I am not taking away your Wisdom, for it has been sanctified by the Great Suffering. Bring it to the abysses, to the place where you, O Sage, will carry your Beacon.

"Return to your Master and tell him that I enjoin him to wait until I come again. Do not go to the One whose name is Silence, for I am always with him. And then come back here and witness My end, for only My end will remove from you the heaviness of the Cold of the Great Cognition..."

Whereupon I, Thales of Argos, stood up and, leaving Clodius of Macedonia at the feet of the Nazarene, slowly bowed to Him and descended from the terrace. On the road, I encountered a group of silent disciples. And here the one who had so rudely greeted me, stepped away from the others and, approaching me, said:

"Sir! If I offended you, I beg you to forgive me."

Upon a more careful examination, I noticed a tinge of enmity and irreconcilability in the depth of his eyes.

"I do not have any hard feelings in my heart, O Judean," I replied. "Remove the animosity burning in your eyes by the Love of your Master. We shall meet with you again when your suffering will be even greater than mine. And meanwhile rejoice, O Judean... at the supreme wisdom of the Great Goddess Pallas Athena, for she, the Great One, has revealed to me that in among your Master's thorns there will also be found your own — a thorn of the utmost betrayal of the Ineffable One!"

The Judean stepped away from me as though he had been stung by a bee. Showing fear, the disciples parted in front of me, Thales of Argos, who was bearing the Cold of the Great Cognition within my dead soul. Only Thomas, along with another young disciple, followed me out of the garden. Here Thomas prostrated himself before me, Thales of Argos, and said in the language of secret knowledge:

"The Great Wisdom of the Theban Sanctuary has now been sanctified in you by the Light of the Ineffable

One, Argive. I bow before it, my foster-mother, for we are brothers therein..."

I stood calmly, and the young disciple touched me, smiling shyly.

"I feel your Great Suffering, Argive, and I am sorry for you. Take this rose from the garden of Magdala. Let it warm your cold heart through the love that I am able to muster. Do not reject my gift, Argive, for this rose has been picked by the Teacher, and we are both His disciples..."

I took the rose, kissed it and, after hiding it next to my chest, I replied:

"For your love I give you my former peace, for it is no longer in my soul. It is close to me — take it. We shall meet with you again, and I shall tell you where the Abode is located, so that you can visit my Master Heraclitus, for I see that your lives converge at one point: his, the great herald of the Wisdom of the Morning Star, and yours, the great Apostle of the Ineffable One! But in one respect you are mistaken: I am not a disciple of your Teacher — I cannot be one, for I know who He is..."

And I left Palestine.

Upon arriving at the secret Abode, I saw my Master, who rushed towards me, greatly disturbed.

"O Argive!" he called. "Our hearts are bound by the chains of the Spirit's life, and so what is this cold of death that is coming from you? My Wisdom could not penetrate beyond the circle of the Great Teacher, and I know nothing about what happened to you. Tell me everything, Argive!"

And I, as I stood next to the column, gradually imparted the whole story to him. And then I saw the Great Heraclitus prostrating himself at my feet.

"Hail to you, Thales of Argos, a wise disciple of mine, who has been sitting at the right hand of God!" he proclaimed. "Thank you for the Great Cross of Waiting that you brought me from Him, the Ineffable One! May His Will be done!"

And I, Thales of Argos, left the Master without regret, for what more could he give to me as one who was carrying the Cold of the Great Prescience within my soul?

I sailed for Pallas and there, in the silence of the Sanctuary of Pelion, I called with a loud voice upon Pallas Athena. And she, the Radiant One, came to me, Thales of Argos, in the night calm of a cool grove, at the roots of the sacred plane tree.

"I have heard the call of the wise son of Hellas, dear to my heart," said the Goddess. What do you need from your Mother, O Son of Wisdom?"

And I again related everything that had happened to me. The Wise One listened to me thoughtfully, and now her motherly hand was resting upon my cold forehead.

"And you, Argive, did you actually come to tell me that you renounce me?" she asked. "So be it! For you, who have sat at the right hand of God, there is no place at my feet. But Argive! Who knows if you will meet my part there when your terrible vision comes true? Will not my eyes flash before you from under the dense veil of a Judean woman?

"Who knows, Argive?! Great is your cold wisdom, O son of Hellas, but after all, we Heavenly Beings still know more than you. Did you not leave Clodius at the feet of the Ineffable One? But how do you know that I did not sit at the same feet before him, at a time when the dawn of life had not yet broken over your planet?

"Look, Argive," said the Wise One as she pointed out to me the Milky Way, "how many gardens of Magdala are scattered throughout Heavenly Palestines? Why could not I have been at one time a humble Mary therein? Think, Argive, you will have enough time, my beloved, wise son, O son of my dear Hellas, who sat at the right hand of God! I accept your renunciation, since I am foreseeing an even greater renunciation maturing in your heart. Truly, you cannot but follow Him, but you will never join those others who follow Him!"

And the hand of the Goddess slightly touched the rose given to me in the garden of Magdala — and the rose blossomed again, and its resurrected love poured into my chest as a warm wave, yet it stopped upon encountering the Cold of the Great Prescience...

The Goddess left, and I remained alone with my thoughts under the shadow of the sacred plane tree. I had broken ties with Wisdom, I had broken ties with the Gods. Only one last connection remained to be broken — the connection with humanity. And I, Thales of Argos, calmly headed towards this final goal.

And so I came once again to Palestine. Here, under the veil of a noble Arab, I met the One who once wisely ruled the Black Race, and who, together with the One whose name is Silence, bowed to the infant Jesus. He was not surprised that I did not render proper veneration to him, the Great One, for all secrets were revealed to him. His gaze that calmly watched the chain of Manvantaras, rested upon me with sympathy.

"Thales of Argos," he said. "I see you are following someone else's path. You who have forever preserved the Beacon of Eternity upon your brow will meet me again in the depths of the spheres of the unmanifested Wisdom of the Cosmos. And we shall work together in the Name of the One at Whose right hand you were sitting in the humble garden of Magdala..."

My friend Empedocles! Should I repeat to you what you already know about the greatest treachery that has ever occurred in the depths of the Universe, about the utmost crime — humanity's crucifixion of their God? No, I shall not repeat this to you. I can only say that at the foot of the cross there was I, Thales of Argos, together with the former Ruler of the Black Race, and the dying gaze of the crucified God rested upon us with inexpressible love. And this gaze melted in me the Cold of the Great Cognition, removing the shackles of ice from my heart, yet it had not changed the decision of my Wisdom.

And in the garden where He was buried and resurrected, I met a humble Judean woman, from under whose dense veil the eyes of the Goddess Pallas Athena glanced at me. Her name was Mary. A disciple of the Crucified One, young John, imparted to me another name of hers, but my lips are pledged to keep the secret of this name.

And I saw that disciple who so rudely spoke to me in the garden of Magdala. He was running, all dripping with perspiration; his eyes were aghast with terror and he was foaming at the mouth. He was roaring like a wild beast. And upon noticing me, he prostrated himself and yelled:

"O wise sir! Help me, for I have betrayed Him and the torments of the whole world are tearing at my heart!"

And I, Thales of Argos, silently handed him a rope and pointed to a nearby tree. He screamed, grabbed the rope, and rushed to the tree... And I watched calmly as all humanity, whom I so much loathed, accepted death in the person of this Judean...

The disciples of the Crucified One asked me to stay with them, but I, Thales of Argos, left and went to the One whose name is Silence, and told him:

"O King and Father! Here I am, Thales of Argos, the son of the free Hellas, an Initiate of the highest degree of the Thebes Sanctuary, a descendant of the royal dynasty of the City of the Golden Gates. I now renounce you, O King and Father, and I renounce humanity. My Wisdom has revealed to me that the Lord of the Element of Air accepts my spirit. Let me go, O King and Father!"

And he let me go, for this incident merited the blessing of the Crucified One.

Many years later I met on the path of my flight a clot of human light. It was my friend Clodius.

He enthusiastically narrated to me how he was crucified in the name of Jesus, how his mother and sisters were tortured on the Earth, and how he, Clodius of Macedonia, himself assisted them in going to the torture...

Then there was no longer the cold of calmness in my elemental heart, and I responded to him:

"Greetings to you, Clodius of Macedonia, O wise disciple of earthly Wisdom and child of human love! But how can I, a poor elementary spirit, not hail you, O light of humanity, for that you, after subjecting your God to crucifixion, imagined you could serve Him by subjecting your mother and sisters, too, to crucifixion and torture! O humanity, pathetic and stiff-necked in your very aspiration to serve the Saviour you yourselves crucified! O children of a snake, how can you be the fledgelings of a dove!"

And thundering and proud of my alienation from accursed humanity, I, Thales of Argos, bounded further ahead amidst a whirlwind and storm.

Meanwhile, the pathetic clot of human light was fearfully making the sign of the cross behind my back. The cross, the cross! Do you really think that the Beacon of Eternity burning in my brow is no purer than your cross which you have stained with great treachery? No, I received it without being stained by a terrible crime, and nothing human, not even your human holiness, can besmirch its pallid, yet noble, elemental light.

Let the peace of the Crucified God be with you, my friend!

**Thales of Argos**

# V. The Way to Calvary

*Thales of Argos to Empedocles,*
*the son of Miles of Athens —*
*at the Supreme Wisdom*
*of the Crucified God — rejoice!*

LISTEN, EMPEDOCLES, and I shall tell you a great true story about those who set out on the way on the fatal day of the crucifixion of God, as well as about someone who is still taking this way and will do so until the day when everything that the Crucified One foretold about the last day of the planet Earth is fulfilled.

Wide was the road which the Divine Sacrifice followed to Calvary, for wide is any way leading to suffering and narrow is any path towards bliss. Oppressive heat caused the clay ground strewn with potholes and hardened deep wheel-ruts to incandesce. In the deathly silence of midday sultriness, the air element became still, not daring even to believe what was being done on the Earth...

Along the road moved a huge crowd of people, hooting and howling. Ahead, with measured soldier's steps, marched a dispassionate elderly centurion, followed by two soldiers. An innumerable crowd of hooting boys surrounded those who came next — three people, battered and dripping with blood, their backs burdened with huge crosses.

I, Thales of Argos, will not describe the One in front, the target of all the mockeries and howls of the surrounding human herd. I will not do this because, in your language, Empedocles, there are neither words nor hues to convey the Divine Love coupled with human suffering that illumined the gentle — yet at the same time unhumanly wise — face of the Galilean. The streaks of blood on Him only aggravated the great and terrible secret that overshadowed this face with its invisible and mysterious wings.

He was followed by a giant Idumean, proudly and freely carrying on his shoulders the burden of a huge cross. His big burning eyes looked at the crowd with great contempt — eyes that reflected the dying gazes of dozens of victims fallen at the hand of the most terrible thief on the Tyrian high road. He walked silently, dripping with sweat and blood. And only occasionally, when the crowd particularly pressed the One in front, would he let out a thick, wild roar of a lion intoxicated with blood — and the crowd would dash aside, while the Roman soldiers walking on the sides would shudder and give a firm squeeze on the hilts of their swords.

Fully bent to the ground under the weight of the cross, a third man was barely crawling behind them. Blood and sweat mixed with the tears on his face. However, these were not tears of despair — they were tears of disgusting cowardice. He was howling dismally, like a hunted hyena, loudly complaining all the time about the injustice of the court that sentenced him to shameful capital punishment for a trifling crime. And on his face with bleary, suppurating eyes were clearly visible the vices and degradation of the whole world, coupled with the most miserable and most loathsome fear for his life.

The crowd thronging behind, like any human herd, was stinking and stupid. There were loafers, barely recovering from a night's drinking bout, countless numbers of beggars, fanatics, frenetically screaming about the blasphemy of the One walking in front and gloatingly mocking Him. Those were simply indifferent animals, rejoicing at the upcoming spectacle. There were harlots, flaunting the luxuriousness of their garments and false tints of their faces. And among them there was a group of important, finely clothed people, seriously discussing the necessity of putting to death the insolent Nazarene who dared reproach the pre-eminent class in their state and radically undermine all respect for it. Those were the Sadducees.

Only occasionally in the crowd could one glimpse pale, thoughtful, exhausted, slovenly dressed scribes — scientists, on whose faces it was possible to read the agonizing efforts to solve the unsolved mystery: Why did the great and wise Caiaphas appear so grievous at last night's meeting of the Sanhedrin? Why did he give the order to destroy all records of the Teacher of Nazareth who was about to be crucified for no apparent reason — a Teacher who was so well acquainted with the Scriptures and the prophets; a Teacher, who was so respected by the all-wise Nicodemus and Gamaliel? And finally and most importantly, what was Caiaphas whispering about for so long and sadly in a corner of the courtyard with John, a young disciple of the One to be crucified? And what did Caiaphas' last words mean:

"Venerable brothers, the chosen of Israel! The Sadducees demand the execution of Jesus of Nazareth, called the Christ among the people. If we do not accede to their demand, they will accuse us before the governor of Judea of being like-minded with Him — One who rejects nobility, wealth, gentility, and merits in matters of state and who preaches poverty and misery. The Romans will suspect us of wanting to revolt, disband the Sanhedrin, impose even greater taxes on the people, and eventually they will crucify the Nazarene anyway. And so, brethren, is it not better if one person dies for the people?"

All this is true, the scribes thought, but why then destroy the records of the great deeds of the Nazarene? What would they say if they were present at the secret meeting of the great, unfamiliar Sanhedrin? This body consisted of twelve Chaldeans who had lost count of years. They were sanctified by the sign of the Great Spirit of the Lunar Initiation of the mysterious Adonai, who reigned in Babylon under the name of the god Bel.

Then could be heard the voice of the same Caiaphas, sounding perplexed, without his usual confidence, as he spoke to the Sanhedrin:

"Initiates of the God of Abraham, Isaac, and Jacob, the children of Adonai, blessed be His Name! The terrible hour has come, which we did not expect. Our Wisdom is powerless; our stars are silent; our elemental forces are mute. The Earth is dumb; in the Holy of Holies of the temple I cannot elicit a reply from the Great Sanctuary of the Moon.

"Brethren! We have been left alone with our Wisdom before the great mystery of an ordinary carpenter from Nazareth. Brethren! From all the corners of the Earth, I have gathered you for the great council, because the great hour is approaching in the lives of the people we protect. This is known to us. What should we do, brethren? How can we save the people and how should we deal with the strange riddle of the Nazarene carpenter?"

For a long time, the assembly was silent, deep in thought, stroking their bushy beards. And then stood up the great Chaldean Daniel, who was the first priest of Babylon and trusted by mighty kings:

"Brethren! I, too, cannot tell you anything. My foresight is silent, there are no revelations from the bright spirits of Adonai; there is no solution in the writings of the mysterious Kabbalah. Who is this Jesus? Is he the One Whom the entire world is waiting for, or is he a stranger, an unknown creation of the depths of another Cosmos? How can we find out? Mysterious and great are his deeds; yet his teaching is so unusual and unexpected, which freely gives away frightening secrets of the Ancient Wisdom for study by the masses. But we are called upon to keep the secrets of this Wisdom. And so, who is he: the greatest criminal in the Cosmos or, terrible as it might be to say, God? And who shall we be if we either oppose or help him?

"This is the dreadful hour for us, brethren, who have been abandoned by Adonai, blessed be His Name! Let all the powers of your Wisdom be harnessed, brethren, for it is clear that not without reason have we been left on our own. Indeed, this question must be resolved through the Wisdom of the Earth alone!"

At this point the wise Chaldean, Rabbi Israel from Nineveh, stood up and said:

"Brethren, wise is our representative in the secular Sanhedrin, Caiaphas! I see there, behind the curtain, three representatives of the other Sanctuaries of the Ancient Wisdom. He has invited them here. I approve this action of his, and although the rules of our Sanctuary of the Moon forbid us to make use of someone else's Wisdom, the hour is too great and threatening not to forgo the letter. I see the signs of two sages; only the sign of the third is obscure to me. Brethren! Let us ask them to speak during this menacing hour. Let another's Wisdom strengthen our own!"

Through silent nodding, the council expressed their approval for the words of the wise Rabbi Israel and for the action of the even wiser Caiaphas. From behind the curtain three came forward, namely: I, Thales of Argos, the Great Initiate of the Theban Sanctuary, the bearer of the Beacon of Eternity; wise Thomas, an Initiate of the Triangle and a disciple of the Nazarene; and the third — though he had no sign, he was altogether shining with a mysterious blue light; his face was hidden from prying eyes by a white veil.

Thomas was the first to speak. In a soft, quiet voice he said:

"O Sons of Lunar Wisdom! I cannot say anything, for my triangle has been laid at the feet of the One Who will be raised on the cross another day. Brethren in earthly Wisdom! I am a disciple of the Nazarene, and it is not for me to tell you about Him…"

The heads of the Sanhedrin silently bowed before the simple words of Thomas. Humbly and quietly he stepped aside. I, Thales of Argos, took his place.

"We, who are present, should rejoice at the Wisdom of the Great Father and Son of Wisdom, Heraclitus!" Thus I began. "The Beacon of Eternity burning on my brow — the Beacon ignited by Hermes the Thrice-Greatest, illumined for me the depths of the Cosmos and I, Thales of Argos, the Great Initiate of the Theban Sanctuary, have comprehended the Great Mystery from Nazareth!"

All twelve Chaldeans stood up together, as well as Thomas, the disciple of the Nazarene, and the One whose countenance was concealed by the white veil, and bowed low to me.

"Greetings to the Great Wisdom of the Theban Sanctuary," a quiet whisper swept through the hall.

"However," I said authoritatively, "the Mystery comprehended by me is a Secret, yet it is not a Secret of the Earth, but a Secret of the Cosmos and Chaos. And you are aware that such Truths cannot be imparted, but must be comprehended. This is why I am silent. I can only tell you that the Cold of the Great Prescience has frozen me, and the terrible mystery of the Cosmos and Chaos has destroyed even my love for the Great Beacon of Eternity burning on my forehead! I have said it all…"

Astounded and perplexed, the Chaldeans jumped up from their seats. Again the strident voice of the wise Daniel resounded:

"Brethren! Great words have we heard just now, but they have frozen my heart. What is this terrible Secret that has seized with cold the mighty heart of the Great Initiate? What is this terrible Secret that was able to suppress the cosmic love of the Great Initiate for the Sign of his Initiation? Intensify your caution, O wise Chaldeans!"

And now in my place was already standing the third speaker. His white veil was thrown back, and there looking at the assembly were a pair of dark eyes, deep like an abyss, on a swarthy, wise face, calm as the noon sky of Hellas.

"O Great Arraim!" whispered Daniel as he prostrated himself before the King and Initiate of the Black. The rest followed him as well; even Thomas knelt on one knee. Only I, Thales of Argos, the Great Initiate of Thebes, a descendant of the royal dynasty of the City of the Golden Gates, remained motionless. For what did the grandeur of the Earth mean to me — me who carried in my heart the Cold of the Great Cognition?

"O Chaldeans," resounded the metallic, calm voice of Arraim — a voice as powerful as an elemental force. "Listen to me. You who have now been abandoned by your protector and left face to face with your Wisdom alone, must find your own way out of the situation. Though the Great Initiate of the Theban Sanctuary, Thales of Argos, has comprehended Truth himself, he cannot convey it to you, for Truth is not something that can be imparted — it must be comprehended.

"You need to follow the middle road — and absolutely leave the decision to the will of the Ineffable One. Do not help with anything and do not oppose anything.

Let the will of the One be done. If you have not comprehended the enigma of Jesus the Nazarene, then view Him as a human being. Destroy all records of His Teaching, life, and deeds. For if all this is from the Ineffable One, then He, the One and Only, will indeed make sure His work does not fade away. And if it be not from Him, then it will all die away, for you yourselves know that only good seed can bear good fruit. And so, there, in the depths of the ages, you will, perhaps, find the solution to the Mystery of the carpenter from Nazareth..."

The whole assembly was enveloped in silence. The Chaldeans spent a long time contemplating Arraim's words, as they stroked their bushy beards.

"So be it!" Daniel finally exclaimed, and all, as one, stood up. After bowing again before Arraim, they left the council venue one by one.

Now, Empedocles, let us go back to the beginning of my story. The Sun was blazing in the sky, as if attempting to melt the sinful Earth. The crowd seemed to have become lazy, trying to walk where occasionally some trees could be found. Finally, close to Calvary itself, the crowd approached a long row of large houses immersed in the greenery of luxurious gardens. Those were the mansions of wealthy Sadducees. Beside one of them stood a group of women, apparently waiting for the arrival of the crowd, and among them was John, a young disciple of the Nazarene. They all were surrounding a tall woman in great suffering, her face tightly veiled. Yet through the veil, I recognized the eyes of the Great Mother — the Mother with whom I, Thales of Argos, once spoke as well. I shall tell you about this meeting later, Empedocles, when, provided the grace of the Ineffable One be with you, you become wiser. For I shall impart to you Great Mysteries, my old friend, which your current mind is not able to comprehend.

When the cedar tree spreading as a canopy over this whole group cast a hospitable shadow on the face of the Divine Convict and when, at the same time, the marvellous eyes of His suffering Mother illumined Him, He staggered and fell to one knee. Hideous loud laughter and mockeries of the crowd rang in everyone's ears. Screeching curses from the third convicted man crashed upon Him. And only the second — the giant thief — almost with tenderness bent over Him and used one of his hands to support the edge of the cross which weighed heavily on the Nazarene.

"O great Argive!" resounded the quiet voice of Arraim next to me. "Can you see an early rising of the Divine Seed in the eyes of this bloodthirsty thief?"

Upon seeing the throng come to a halt, the centurion walking in front came closer. His stern soldier's gaze surveyed the crowd.

"Jerusalemite swine!" he said in a stentorian voice. "He was given to you for your amusement, and you have the right to crucify Him, but He is going to death, and I shall not allow you to taunt Him. He is exhausted; His cross is larger than that of others. Will anyone help Him?"

The crowd became torpid. What? To carry the cross of One convicted? And thereby to accept a part of His shame?

Who of the faithful Judeans could agree to this?

"I swear by Osiris! You're right, soldier!" suddenly reverberated in someone's thunderous voice, and a man with a broad and thick greying beard pushed his way commandingly through the crowd. "You're right, soldier! Only vile Judeans could scoff at the suffering of a person who, as I've heard, was convicted to please the rich. Stand up, my friend, I'll carry your cross, even if it is made of lead. I swear by Osiris and Isis, or else I'm not the blacksmith Simon from Cyrene!"

The giant grabbed the cross of the Saviour, and slung it over his shoulder with a single swing of his arm. Yet at the same moment his eyes flashed with the fire of amazement.

"But it really *is* made of lead!" he mumbled. "How could He have carried it so far?"

"Great Argive!" I again heard Arraim's voice. "Count carefully! The thief from Phœnicia, the soldier from Rome, and the coarse blacksmith from Egypt! What will you say about the Great Sowing of the humble carpenter from Galilee?"

Suddenly, the group of women was moved apart by someone's white, imperious hand, and next to the Divine Sufferer appeared an elderly, tall, thin Judean in the luxurious clothes of a rich Sadducee. His eyes glistened with wild malice; he angrily grabbed the Galilean by the shoulder and pushed Him forward.

"Go! Go!" was the only thing he could articulate at that moment, choking as he was with spite and rage.

Gently the Saviour looked at him.

"Greetings to you, Ahasuerus!" He whispered almost inaudibly, His lips reeking with blood. After slowly rising from the dust, He followed Simon who was bearing His cross; He went, quietly leaning on the thief's friendly hand, which was stretched out to Him. Yelling and making a great deal of noise, the crowd moved after them; the group of women started to move as well. Ahasuerus remained alone near the gate of his gorgeous mansion, continuing to vomit revilings and curses in the wake of the Convicted One.

At once Arraim stepped out in front of him. I could not recognize him: this was no longer a humble pilgrim, this was no longer a scientist teaching wisdom to wise Chaldeans — this was the Great High Priest of the Radiant One, His fiery servant, who gathered within himself all the great magical powers of the planet. His eyes glared with the irresistible force of Chaos, and an inexpressible chilling horror fettered the body of the vile Ahasuerus. Slowly, but slowly, Arraim raised his hand.

"Ahasuerus!" his voice resounded like steel. "I say to you in your own words: Go! Go! Go, until He returns again! Go! From the East to the West lies your way! Go! Each century I give you three days to rest. And let your mind be always active! Go! Examine, learn, and repent! Go! Here is my curse to you — from Arraim, the King and Father of the Black! Go! In the name of the One who is known as Silence, the Great High Priest of the Ineffable One, I say to you: Go!"

And then Ahasuerus shuddered as if in a dream, staggered, and went. He is still going, Empedocles. I saw him in the taiga of Siberia, and in the streets of Paris, and on the peaks of the Andes, and in the sands of the Sahara, and in the ice of the North Pole.

Bent over, with a long, flowing beard and burning eyes, he moves at a steady pace from pole to pole, from the East to the West — he keeps going, grown wise with great wisdom and no less great repentance.

Now, sometimes, he is not alone when he walks. The eyes of the Initiate are able to discern next to him a white figure, resplendent with a gentle blue light, as though leading old Ahasuerus by the hand. This figure whispers to him something softly and tenderly, and the eyes of the Wandering Jew become wet with scorching tears, and his pale, parched lips whisper:

"O my Lord and my Saviour!"

Strange things I have told you, Empedocles, my friend. Some day, when the holy fire of life still glimmers in you and my elemental heart can remember the past without trembling, I shall tell you about the last moments of God in a human form.

May my peace be with you, my friend Empedocles!

**Thales of Argos**

# VI. The Mother of God

*Thales of Argos to Empedocles,*
*the son of Miles of Athens —*
*at the Supreme Wisdom*
*of the Eternally Young*
*Virgin-Mother — rejoice!*

A T SOME POINT, Empedocles, I did not find it necessary to tell you that I did not immediately leave
Palestine after the meeting in the garden of Magdala had
inundated my heart with the Cold of the Great Prescience.

I, Thales of Argos, felt with my whole being that the
deepest secrets of the combination of the Fiery Veil with
all existence manifested in the Cosmos still had not been
fully grasped by my Wisdom. I felt that the Mystery of
God's manifestation in human form could not be comprehended by me until I understood the Source of Life that
had brought the Divine flesh into existence. And I needed
to comprehend this, for I realized that, no matter how
terrible might have been the Cold of the Great Prescience
that had frozen my wise heart, the depths of the Supreme
Wisdom still lying on my cosmic path had to be explored
in full. The Great Initiate could not stop half-way.

Quiet and deserted were the intricate, curved, and
dusty streets of little Nazareth when I, Thales of Argos,
set my foot upon them in the mysterious light of the rising
Selene. Painted little houses that hid the peaceful population were planted around with olive trees. I, Thales of
Argos, did not need to ask the way, for I saw a pillar of
the faint blue light rising from one of the houses directly
to Heaven, becoming lost there amidst stellar roads. This
was the light of a special hue, characteristic of the source of
Great Life — the light of Female Deities, the light which

illumined the head of the Eternally Young Virgin-Mother in Atlantis and surrounded the appearance of the Divine Isis in the Sanctuaries of Thebes.

Quietly, yet confidently, I knocked at the door of this little house. The door opened at once, and on the threshold appeared a tall woman, whose slender shape was lost in the wide folds of her plain, coarse dress. Her face was hidden under rough Phœnician muslin.

"What do you want, traveller?" resounded in the lower chest tones of her voice, which immediately reminded me of the sound of the silver strings of the sistrum in the temple of the Divine Isis.

"I'm a foreigner, Mother," I replied. "I'm seeking rest and food. Is it the custom with the children of Adonai to accept a weary traveller at such a late hour?"

"I'm only a poor widow, sir," a quiet answer followed. "Teachers in our synagogue condemn single women receiving travellers, and I'm alone, as the sons of my late husband work in the fields near Bethlehem for the wealthy Sadducees, and my only son..." here the woman stammered, "has left for Jerusalem. Yet I lack the spirit to refuse you, O weary traveller, and if a mug of goat's milk and a flat cake will satisfy you, then..."

"Then I'll call God's blessing upon you, Mother," I replied. "A few days ago, I saw your Son, Mother, and spoke with Him..."

"Did you really speak with him? What did he...?" She moved impulsively towards me, but stopped right away. "Forgive me, O traveller, forgive this mother, worrying about her only son... Come in, take a rest, and eat..."

I, Thales of Argos, entered the more than humble dwelling place of the Mother of God. There were two benches, a large table, a pitiful and miserable bed of reeds in the corner, a spinning wheel over by a curved window,

and an old candlestick on a small shelf in the corner —
those were the only decorations in the New Temple
which, I, Thales of Argos, entered.

She hastily put on the table a large earthen mug of
milk, along with a flat cake, black from the charcoal ad-
hering to it, and, after bowing to me, said:

"Taste, sir, our bread..."

I, too, bowed, sat down at the table and, after casting
a keen gaze at the woman standing in front of me, said:

"Blessed be your bread, Mother; I have already drunk
your milk..."

The woman raised her head.

"Have you already been to see us, sir?" She asked.

A new and terrible riddle of the existence of the Ineffable One resounded for me from Her lips.

But could I, Thales of Argos, the Great Initiate of
Thebes, bearing the sign of the Beacon of Eternity on my
brow and the Cold of the Great Prescience in my heart,
retreat before the mysteries of Existence? I strained my
powers and enveloped her with the warmth of my Wisdom, which at the same time concealed the breath of
Mother Isis...

The woman gave a start and sat down opposite me
on the bench.

"You called God's blessing on my house, sir," She said,
"and it is indeed so, for I immediately felt a calm in my
heart. Did you see my son and talk with him?"

"I saw Him and talked with Him, Mother," I answered, "and He blessed me. What can my call — the
call of a pathetic worm of the earth — for God's blessing
on the house of the Mother of Jesus, the carpenter from
Nazareth, possibly mean compared to *His* blessing?"

The woman shuddered.

"Did you... did you believe in him, sir? Did he not take you as one of his disciples?" She asked softly but impetuously.

"No, Mother," I replied. "I don't believe in Him, for I have recognized Him. And it is not for me to be His disciple, for I always, from now on and forever will be a pitiful servant of His..."

"Your speech is strange, sir," She uttered after a pause. "However, in your face I read wisdom and great suffering, and my heart — the heart of a poor, miserable widow — feels sympathy for you and is drawn to you. Tell me, O wise foreigner, whom do you consider my son to be?"

"And whom do you yourself consider Him to be, Mother?" I, Thales of Argos, responded with a question.

The woman sighed and began to finger the corners of her veil.

"You, sir," She said, "seem to have brought with you the breath of my son... It is as though he were here... And my heart is full of trust towards you... All my life I've been tormented by the question you asked, and, believe it or not, sir, the answer to it sometimes frightens me. Who is my son? Do you think I know this, sir? But can my feeble mind — the mind of a woman — understand everything that has happened on my humble path?"

And in a soft, hurried whisper She began to impart to me, Thales of Argos, marvellous plain descriptions of her pure childhood in a family of simple, pure-hearted parents; of the miraculous invisible voices which were constantly whispering strange and wondrous passages in her ear; of her extraordinary dreams; of a winged light-bearing youth who appeared to her and proclaimed to her the words of Good Tidings; of her chaste marriage and immaculate, virgin birth of a Son, who, after His coming into the world, was worshipped by three men of kingly mien.

"They were like you, sir," She said, "not in the face, no, but in the great peace that they exhaled and by the same quality of wisdom which I see in you... Only, my dear unknown traveller, they didn't have on their foreheads any wrinkles of great suffering..."

"And what happened next?"

Once again words flowed about the early wisdom of the wonderful Child; about the miracles occurring around Him or which He Himself performed; about His great love for all that exists...

Only one thing, it seemed, the Mother Herself did not understand: that inexpressible Cosmic Love with which She Herself was imbuing Her words about Her Son... And in the heat of the conversation, She threw back the veil from Her face, and — glory be to the Name of the Eternally Young Virgin-Mother! — I, Thales of Argos, beheld marvellous, refined features, including eyes whose depth dispelled my doubts, yet all the while, it seemed, deepening even more the infinite mystery that had opened wide before me.

"Mother," I enquired, "don't you believe that your Son is the Messiah foretold by the prophets and Moses? And maybe," I quietly added, "even greater than the Messiah?"

The woman glanced at me fearfully.

"But... he's a human being, sir," She whispered in bewilderment.

"However, you, too, are an ordinary woman, Mother," I replied. "After all, nothing physical distinguishes you from your sisters. Or, perhaps, you, Mother, have not told me everything?"

The woman lowered her head shyly.

"There's just one thing," She said, "that confuses my heart, sir. I'm a sincerely faithful Judean, diligently following all the instructions of the Law and our teachers... but... my dreams perplex me..."

"I'm a dream interpreter from Egypt," I said quickly. "Tell me your dreams, Mother, and I'll try to explain them to you..."

"Really?!" the woman exclaimed joyfully. "Blessed be your arrival, sir! Perhaps you will remove the heaviness of ignorance from my soul..."

And timidly, as though She were ashamed, She began to tell me her dreams. Right from her very first words, a dawn of great understanding flared up in my mind. Before my mind's gaze, amidst the thunder of cosmic elemental forces and sighs of emerging worlds, flashed images of the inexpressibly grand life of the all-powerful Great Goddess.

This was the Goddess whose breast suckled ever new Cosmoses; the Goddess whose Divine heel imperiously trampled down the debris of the old ones; the Goddess who arranged the existence of the gloomy depths of Chaos; the Goddess who listened to the prayers of hundreds of billions of countries, peoples, humanities, and evolutions; the Goddess who commanded legions of light-bearing spirits, whose radiant gaze caused the Lord of Darkness to flee; the Goddess who heard my voice — the voice of the Great Hierophant in the temple of the Eternally Young Virgin-Mother...

And it was so wondrous for me, Thales of Argos, to listen to these stories from the trembling lips of an ordinary, poor, humble widow of a miserable carpenter from Judea...

"Tell me, Mother," I asked, "have you ever told your Son about these dreams?"

"I have," the woman replied in a barely audible voice.

"And what did you hear from Him, Mother?"

"His answer was strange," She replied. "He lovingly said to me: 'Forget your marvellous visions for the time being, Mother. But there is no sin in them, for they are from the Lord.' And he also said this: 'When your cross finishes, Mother, which you accepted for Me, you will return to the life of your dreams...' But what that means, I don't know..."

"Tell me, Mother," I enquired again, "do you happen to remember me amidst your visions?"

The woman carefully looked me over and thoughtfully turned Her limitless gaze to a dark corner of the shack.

"As soon as you came in here, sir," She said quietly, "I felt that you were not a stranger to me. However, so far, I am searching my memory in vain... But... wait... wait..." And She suddenly cast her fathomless eyes on me. "What did your words mean when you said that you had already drunk my milk?"

And She jumped up from her seat, without taking her gaze off me — a gaze which had suddenly blazed up with myriads of suns.

I, Thales of Argos, stood up as well, upon realizing that the great and terrible moment had come — the moment of victory of the Light over the darkness, the Spirit over the flesh, Heaven over the Earth, the Goddess over the woman...

"Wait, I'm remembering..." the woman was saying slowly, and the gentle sounds of the sistrum and silver bells quietly started to resound from the dark corners of the shack. "I see... a temple... I... and you prostrated at my feet... my faithful servant... another temple... and you again — the great and wise one... You... you... are drinking my milk... Thales of Argos, my faithful servant!"

All this escaped from Her lips like some kind of ringing chord, and at the same moment I fell at the feet of the Great Goddess Isis incarnated in a human form...

For a long time I, Thales of Argos, was lying down, not daring to raise my head, for I considered myself unworthy to contemplate the countenance of the awakening Goddess. The sounds of marvellous ethereal melodies were spreading and growing more and more intense. And only sometimes it seemed to me that dominant in them was some majestic, yet sad and grievous tone, as if the whole Cosmos were complaining to God about its forlornness without the Goddess-Mother who had gone off no one knew whereto.

"Get up, Thales of Argos, rise, my beloved servant," the voice of the Goddess soughed over me. "Stand up and sit down. Forget Heaven, because we are not here for Heaven, but for the Earth..."

And I, Thales of Argos, stood up and sat down. Everything was the same as before: the shack with its dark corners, and the humble Woman attired in a dress of dark rough cloth with a veil covering Her face.

"Truly strange is your destiny, Argive," continued Isis-Mary. "When I gave you my milk to drink, I myself didn't know that you were predetermined to play a part in my deeds and existence: to appear at the instant my earthly dream was to end. But it is finished, and from now on I'm aware that the hour for which I indeed came to the Earth, is near.

"You know what hour I'm talking about, Argive — it is the hour from whose foresight your courageous and wise heart has become frozen, son of Hellas. The time of the Great Sacrifice is approaching. And now I've understood which weapon is to pierce my soul — the prophet told me when I ascended the stairs of the temple of

Adonai for the first time... It's horrible, Argive, to have the heart of a loving earthly mother, but it's even more horrible to illumine it with Divine consciousness... So this is the cross about which the One Whom I regarded as my Son told me... This is from where that Great Love has come from — the Great Love which has bound my heart with the manifestation of the Ineffable One."

Silence fell. The head of Isis-Mary was bent low, and Divine thoughts were swirling around Her veil-hidden brow.

"Argive," She quietly continued. "Has your Wisdom prompted you to discover why exactly I am now an ordinary woman, under whose covering no one, except the three and now you, the Hierophant of Egypt, recognizes the Goddess-Mother? My Divine Son had to come to the Earth as a human being, for only a human being can save humanity, and for that He also had to be born from an earthly mother. But nothing was to confuse the gazes and minds of people at the appearance of God incarnated in a human form — and so, by the will of the Ineffable One, I assumed a human body...

"Moreover, Argive, I even gave away my consciousness, exchanging it for the consciousness of an earthly woman, until the time I needed the strength and power of the Goddess in order to accomplish the mission entrusted to me. And from now on I won't let anyone notice my awakening — I'll remain the same Mary until the end of my earthly days, which won't differ from anyone else's end of days...

"In the life of each Virgin-Mother, giving birth to a new Earth, there appears such a moment, Argive, when she, while carrying out her supreme purpose, absorbs the grief and sorrow of everything born of her, and for this moment she needs all her power and wisdom in order to truly remain the Mother of all Creation, for only after giving birth to God can she experience the whole Love of God, which until then was peacefully slumbering in the meadows of the Most High Paradise, in the Garden of Divine Mothers...

"When this terrible moment comes, be there, Argive, near me. Oh, and not to help me, for no one will be able to help me — indeed, they must not — but so that your great Wisdom may become even greater from beholding the two Divine Sacrifices... And now, Argive, gather your Wisdom and evoke the countenance of my Son before me, for I, after waking up from the dream, need the encouragement of His gaze... I myself have no right in any way to go beyond the boundaries or possibilities of a common woman of the Earth..."

And I, Thales of Argos, rose and, after commandingly invoking the crafty spirits of reflection, ordered them to send our images into space and, together with them, I also sent out the fiery arrows of my thoughts. The glints of reflection of roads, fields, gardens, and trees began to oscillate like a whirlwind... then shuddered... and stopped.

And then we saw a lone olive tree among the verdant fields; several people were sleeping peacefully beside it. And one was sitting, bent over a stone nearby. It was He — the Son and God. With a quiet, truly Divine affection, He was looking at His Mother...

"Let the blessing of the Father rest upon you, My awakened Mother," He said. "What has been predestined from the beginning of time of this Earth is now being fulfilled. Come to Jerusalem, Mother, for the goal of the path of Our cross is near..."

And His Divine gaze fixed itself on me.

"You have done everything you had to do, O wise son of the Earth," He said. "Finish the path of your earthly wanderings, for the secrets revealed to you are so great that the Earth will be unable to hold you, Argive. I see the wings unfolding behind your back, O son of Hellas — from star to star you will fly and will bring the Sign of My Cross to the borders of the Universe, preaching My Name and that of My Mother..."

He stretched out His blessing hands, and the vision disappeared.

Once again, I prostrated myself before Mother Isis.

"O Great Mother!" I appealed. "Everything that I have and everything that I shall have — I lay all at Thy feet, O Great Mother. My heart and mind have become frozen, and now I see that I'm poor and don't need anything..."

Gently the hand of Isis-Mary touched me.

"Arise, my servant, arise, O servant of the Ineffable God. What my Son said must be fulfilled. But no wings of yours will ever carry you away from my love and breath, Argive... And now embark on a journey, O wise son of Hellas — we'll meet again at the foot of my Son's cross..."

And I left. The fields were quiet, and the night road was quiet, Selene was streaming her light quietly — and all this was mirrored as glints in the cold heart of the lonely traveller carrying within his breast the terrible Wisdom of Vision...

Only somewhere in the heights, in the blue vault of the sky, were still sounding the strings of an unknown sistrum, as though the angels of the Ineffable One were plucking them with their wings, protecting the peace of Mother Isis incarnated in human form...

Peace to you, Empedocles!

**Thales of Argos**

# VII. At the Foot of the Cross

*Thales of Argos to Empedocles,*
*the son of Miles of Athens —*
*at the Infinite Love*
*of the Crucified God — rejoice!*

ENDLESS AND ETERNAL is the road which I, Thales of
Argos, have travelled among stellar paths, universes,
and cosmoses. The dream of Pralaya shall not touch me.
The chain of Manvantaras is curling before me like mist.
Yet there is no abyss of Chaos, there is no such Eternity
where I could forget even a single moment that I spent at
foot of the cross at Calvary. I shall try to impart to you,
Empedocles — in a deficient human tongue — the story
full of human and imperfect grief.

When I, Thales of Argos, told you, Empedocles, the
account of Ahasuerus, I brought the story to the point
when those condemned to be crucified, surrounded by
a stinking human herd, approached Calvary. At the top
of the hill, a few people were already digging holes for
planting the crosses. Nearby there was a small group of
Sadducees and fanatical priests, who were apparently in
charge of everything. At their order, Simon the Blacksmith lowered the cross of the Galilean into the middle
hole. He wiped off the perspiration rolling like hail down
his face, and said:

"I swear by Osiris! Never have I ever in my life borne
such a weight... But I wouldn't be Simon the Blacksmith,
if I didn't agree to bear this cross until the end of my life,
if only to deliver this gentle human being from suffering!"

"Bless you, Simon," resounded the quiet voice of the
Galilean. "Anyone who has ever carried My Cross, even

for a moment, will experience Eternal Bliss in the Gardens of My Father..."

"I don't understand what you're saying," Simon naïvely answered, "but I feel that there has never been and will never be a better moment in my life. But what have I done? Who are you, O gentle human being, that your words are like cool water in the desert for withered lips?"

"Enough talk!" shrilly shouted some short, spiteful priest with a tousled beard and darting pig eyes, while pushing everyone apart. "Take their clothes off and proceed with the crucifixion!"

These last words were addressed to the Roman soldiers, who stood in a semicircle behind a sullen-looking centurion.

"Do not give orders to those who are not under your command, you Judean," the latter said sharply. "My soldiers are doing their duty regarding these two," he added, pointing to the thief and the money-changer, "for they have been convicted by the proconsul. But as for the poor Nazarene, he is given to you — so do with him whatever you want. No Roman soldier's hand will touch him. But I shall do what I have to do..."

And with these words the centurion turned and made a sign to the soldier who stood directly behind him. That one handed him a wooden plate, painted in a bright red colour, with words inscribed in Hebrew, Greek, and Latin:

"Jesus of Nazareth, the King of the Jews."

The centurion nailed it with a single blow of the hammer to the top of the Galilean's cross. A scream of spiteful indignation burst from the lips of the Sadducees and priests who were standing close by.

"Take it off, soldier, take it off at once!" they shouted, and the small priest even tried to tear off the plate, but was thrown aside by the powerful hand of the centurion.

"By order of Cæsar's governor, Pontius Pilate!" he exclaimed imperiously and raised his hand. "If you don't like the inscription, go to the consul and demand cancellation, yet until then, I swear by Jupiter, I don't advise anyone to prevent a Roman soldier from executing a command given to him! Proceed with your work," he curtly barked the order to his soldiers.

They silently approached the thief and the money-changer. The first himself took off his clothes and lay down on the cross, never tearing his eyes, even for a second, away from the gentle but exhausted visage of the Galilean, who was standing with His hands folded near His cross, His face radiant with some kind of inner light.

A loathsome scene started with the money-changer, who was screaming, whining, and biting the hands of the soldiers who were undressing him.

The small priest, who had already recovered from the centurion's blow, briefly exchanged whispered words with the group of Sadducees. Then he ran up to the centurion and started to say something in a hurry, waving his arms and pointing first at the thief lying on the cross, then at the squealing money-changer. An expression of indescribable disgust and contempt flashed across the brave soldier's face.

"I swear by Jupiter," he muttered through clenched teeth, "how much meanness lies in your soul, you priest! What God do you serve? In your opinion, you are forbidden to shed blood, yet you are allowed to lie, deceive, and betray, aren't you? But you're right: two of these scoundrels are also Judeans, and I don't have any orders in their regard, while you have been appointed as a supervisor of the execution. Do what you want, I won't interfere."

The priest rushed to the soldiers and stopped them. The perplexed thief got up from the cross and stared in bewilderment at the priest and Sadducees who came to him. Then they immediately placed next to him the shivering and half-naked money-changer, who was cowardly looking around like a dog.

"Listen, you!" the priest was shrieking and grimacing in front of them. "We can petition the consul to forgive you, but on the condition that you carry out the execution of that blasphemer," he added, pointing to the Galilean. "We are forbidden to shed blood, and we don't have our own executioners, and the Romans don't want to execute him, for it was not they who convicted him. Well? Will you do it?"

The money-changer at once jumped up and rushed to the feet of the priest.

"Take, take me!" he yelled. "I'll always serve you faithfully!"

The priest nodded his head with approval, grinning slyly.

"Well, and what will you say?" the priest asked the thief.

"You want me to nail him," he said, nodding at the Galilean, "to the cross?"

"Well, yes," confirmed the priest impatiently.

The thief's eyes flashed with anger. He sighed deeply and bitterly spat straight into the eyes of the priest. Then he turned, and after parting the crowd, approached his cross and lay down on it again.

Behind them was heard the approving roar of the centurion:

"I swear by Jupiter! He would make a good soldier."

The priest woke up from the unexpected insult, and his lips watered with the foam of fury and rage.

"Nail him, nail him!" he screeched and, upon running up to the thief lying on the cross, kicked his head with his sandalled foot.

But then the soldiers, following a sign from the centurion, pushed him away and silently set about their dreaded task. Less than three minutes later, the huge cross, with the large bloody body of the thief hanging on it, seemed to rise rather sorrowfully above the crowd before sinking heavily into the ground. Not a single groan escaped from the tightly closed lips of the man being executed: on his face, twisted in suffering, only his eyes were burning brightly, gazing relentlessly at the Galilean.

And He raised His hand and whispered something softly, as if blessing the thief.

And my eyes — the eyes of an Initiate in the highest degree — clearly saw someone's gentle, barely noticeable (even for me) wings spread above the head of the thief pinnacled on the cross and lovingly fluttering over him...

The disgusting money-changer was already making a fuss around the motionless Galilean and tearing off His clothes.

He interspersed this hellish activity with the vilest curses and taunts, glancing askance at those around, as though trying to win the approval of the crowd by his behaviour.

However, the faces of the Sadducees and priests were burning with hypocrisy and malice, while the faces of the soldiers were gloomy and morose. The crowd huddled around him, restrained only by the semicircle of soldiers.

"Argive!" said Arraim, who was standing next to me. "The moment of the Great Sacrifice is nearing. Can you sense how Nature has fallen silent from horror?"

And it was true: life, it seemed, was in full swing only in the crowd at Calvary — everything else around had become frozen in some sort of stupor: neither a breath of wind, a flight of birds, nor a crackling of insects, could be detected; the Sun turned red, but his increasingly strong rays seemed to become hotter, more sultry and suffocating; and a kind of gloomy, sinister haze could be seen approaching from the horizon.

"Look, Argive!" the voice of Arraim was heard again.

And here against the darkened background of blue-black sky, I, Thales of Argos, suddenly beheld someone's mournful eyes, full of such inexpressible and inhuman anguish that my soul, frozen in the Cold of the Great Cognition, shuddered from learning the indescribable secret Mystery of Divine Sorrow.

And I, Thales of Argos, whose spirit had been akin to the calm of basalt rocks in the depths of the ocean, now felt the scorching tears of my eyes melting the ice of my heart...

Those were the eyes of the same God that people hanged on the cross.

And here the shriek of the money-changer broke through with its nasty howling discord. The priest had deceived him and now the Roman soldiers were bitterly tormenting him...

The very next moment, the three crosses overshadowed the summit of Calvary...

"For it was said: 'And He was numbered with the transgressors.' " These words I heard uttered right beside me. Upon turning, I saw young John, whose eyes, overflowing with tears, were fixed his Teacher and God.

Flooded with the marvellous light of love, my soul could not refrain any longer, and I impulsively took hold of his hand. He was startled and looked at me in amazement.

"O wise Hellene!" he said. "That is where we were to meet with you... You predicted this, O Sage. I know you love my Teacher. Could you ask the Roman to permit the Mother of my Lord to approach His cross?"

But just as soon as I was about to fulfil John's request, I noticed the centurion coming towards us, together with Arraim.

"This noble Ethiopian," he said, pointing to the latter, "has arrived from Pontius Pilate with an order for me to grant the desire of the mother of the crucified 'King of the Jews.' He told me that she was here with you, O disciple of the Crucified One. Where is she and what does she want? I swear by Jupiter! I'll do everything I can and even more, for never has my soul hurt so much as now, at the sight of this heinous execution of one who is innocent..."

"Look," he added, as he angrily pointed to the group of Sadducees and priests, who were abhorrently grimacing in a sort of satanic gloat at the foot of the cross, "just look! I've seen a lot in my lifetime, but, may lightning strike me, I've never seen a denser blood than that shed today, nor a viler group of people than your compatriots, O disciple of the Crucified One!"

He turned away and spat on the ground with loathing.

"We should like to ask you, O centurion, to allow the Mother of our Teacher to approach His cross," John said softly.

"So that she might hear all the taunts and scoffs which these children of Tartarus hail down upon the head of her suffering son?" the Roman centurion asked.

"However, I'll help you in this cause. Invite the woman to come here, and come with her yourself," he said as he went over to the cross.

"Enough!" he shouted in a stentorian voice.

"Your job has been done. Your 'King' is hanging on the cross. Go away from here. Give place to the sacred tears of the mother!"

Angrily glancing askance at the centurion and grumbling with displeasure, the Sadducees and priests rushed back from the cross.

With quiet step, leaning on John's arm, the veiled Woman approached the cross and fell with mute sobbing at the bloodied feet of the Crucified One.

The eyes of God looked down with Divine gentleness, suffering with human anguish.

"John!" a quiet voice resounded.

"I entrust to you My Mother: Give her to them... Mother! Descend from Thy heights and come to them..."

And the eyes of the Saviour rose again and stopped at the group consisting of Arraim and the centurion, along with me, Thales of Argos.

I inadvertently glanced at Arraim. Turning his eyes to the Saviour, the most powerful Magician on the Earth was all outburst and aspiration. I realized that with just one sign from the cross, everything around could have been incinerated by the terrible Fire of Space...

But from the cross came only a quiet sound:

"Father! Forgive them, for they know not what they do..."

The head of Arraim, the Great Magician of the planet, bowed low at this reproach.

"I swear by Jupiter!" the centurion beside me whispered in amazement. "He forgives them! Yes, he is truly the Son of God!"

I, Thales of Argos, eagerly watched everything, for my heart was now brimming over with the stream of Divine

Love instead of the Cold of the Great Cognition. And I saw how the eyes of God turned to the thief who, in unspeakable agony, had still not torn his gaze away from the Lord. Either a moan or a growl was a response to the look of God.

"Where is your Kingdom, O crucified King?" — these words burst painfully from the torn chest of the thief. "Wherever you are, O gentle one, take me with yourself, too!"

"Today you will be with Me in My Kingdom," — was the silent answer heard from the cross.

And again, I saw invisible wings begin to flutter over the head of the first chosen of God — the thief from the high road. And when a kind of shadow fell upon his face, he gave a deep sigh, his head lowered to his chest.

"I swear by Jupiter!" the centurion standing beside me whispered in confusion. "What marvellous things are happening today? But it appears that he is already dead!"

"Look, Argive!" Arraim said to me with a special solemnity, as his hand fell upon my shoulder.

Then the haze, which had long ago started to gather on the horizon, drew closer and became gloomier. And I, Thales of Argos, saw how two black wings grew from it, similar to bat wings; how two huge blood-red eyes opened; how someone's mighty and proud brow, like the breath of Chaos, took shape with an inverted triangle on top of it. And then this unknown and incredibly heavy "something" all descended on Calvary.

A terrible crash of thunder burst forth in the haze, and the earth responded to it with the shock of a powerful quake.

With a roaring howl, the human crowd, petrified with horror, rushed to flee wherever they could in the darkness, falling into ruts and pits, crushing against each other, and knocking one another down.

Meanwhile, the black haze coiled into a round gigantic mass, like a Serpent's body, and slowly crept to Calvary — O wonder of wonders of the Cosmos! The head with blood-red eyes clung to the bloodied feet of the Crucified One. And my ears — the ears of the Great Initiate — heard a peculiar harmony of Chaos, as though rising like distant peals of thunder from the unknown depths of Creation. That was the voice of Gloom itself, the voice of the Great Lord of Matter Unmanifest in the Spirit. He said:

"Bright Brother! You who took my servant to yourself, take his Master to yourself as well..."

"Come, Sufferer!" came a barely audible answer from the cross.

"And the seed of the woman crushed the Serpent's head!" I heard the metallic whisper of Arraim. "The Great Sacrament of Reconciliation has occurred. Look, Argive!"

And right there, in front of my eyes, such a marvellous scene unfolded which I shall never see again, even if billions of Great Cycles of Creation flashed before me.

The Great Light blazed up, and its shaft, as wide as the horizon, rose up to Heaven. And in this shaft of Light, I saw the head of the Crucified One, so divinely beautiful, illumined with such an indescribable expression of Divine Love that could not be reproduced even by archangelic choirs.

And then next to the head of God, which by now had departed from the flesh, another head took shape, magnificent with proud, though human, beauty. Traces of great suffering were not yet smoothed on it, and signs of a cosmic struggle had not yet disappeared from it. However, the eyes no longer were blood-red, but shone with the depths of the noon sky, burning with a love beyond people's knowledge, and directed to Christ the Victor.

"This is the birth of a new Archangel." whispered Arraim.

And instantly, between these two gigantic figures, a little white clot of light fluttered, joyfully gliding over the chest of the Lord. It was the liberated soul of the thief from the Tyrian high road.

And it seemed that the string of a giant harp broke in the Heavens, and a quiet sound flitted over the Earth:

It happened!

The body of the beheaded Serpent crawled away from the hill, dispersing in space and becoming lighter.

Overwhelmed with what had occurred, I approached the cross together with Arraim and, upon looking up at the Crucified One, I saw His eyes — still alive, yet the Spirit was not in them. This was only human flesh, suffering, infinitely kind, infinitely loving, infinitely enlightened, but, alas, only human. The Spirit had departed from it, leaving agonizing loneliness to the last. And the flesh moaned:

"My God, why hast Thou forsaken me?"

"I swear by Jupiter! I can't take this any more!" the centurion beside me shouted hoarsely and, snatching a spear from the arms of a soldier who was as pale as death, he thrust it vehemently into the side of the Crucified One.

"I may have acted against my oath in lessening His suffering," said the centurion, staring at me with a half-crazed look, "but what I witnessed today not even Augustus himself could endure!

"What was that haze, those voices, who was this executed man? — tell me, O wise Ethiopian!" he asked Arraim in a trembling voice.

"You yourself said recently, soldier, that it was the Son of God," Arraim replied.

With his hands outstretched in perplexity, the coarse Roman centurion kept staring at the face of the Galilean, already covered with the shadow of death, with an agonized expression of questioning — like looking at a puzzle with no solution.

I turned around, slowly, and examined everything I could see. Only two soldiers, both looking pale and terrified to death, remained on their feet — all the rest were lying face down on the ground. The crowd had dispersed. Not far away lay the corpse of the short priest, his face covered with a bloody foam. At the Cross of the Lord the woman could still be seen clinging to the feet of the Crucified One, along with John, who, sad yet enlightened, was entirely immersed in prayer. The powerful figure of the Roman soldier was standing right in front of the cross, along with two Sons of Wisdom — Arraim and me. This was the setting of God's last minutes on the Earth.

Life was still glimmering in the body of the pathetic money-changer. After coming to his senses, the centurion ordered a soldier to break his shins, while he himself thoughtfully stepped aside.

At this time, from the nearby bushes began to appear the pale faces of women and the Galilean's disciples. I recognized Mary Magdalene and Peter. Upon noticing me, Mary ran up to me and asked, her face drowning in tears:

"O wise Hellene! Could He really die?"

"He will rise again, Mary," I answered and, seeing her suffering, embraced her with the warmth of my Wisdom.

She gave a shudder and straightened up.

"I knew He would! Thank you, Sage!" she whispered, ran up to the cross, and fell at the feet of the Crucified One from the other side.

The centurion was absently staring at the whole scene.

"I swear by Jupiter! I don't know what to do," he muttered.

"Don't be confused, brave soldier," Arraim said to him, taking his hand. "I know Pontius Pilate has only honourable intentions — he is my friend — and believe me, your mercy towards the women and the disciples of the Crucified One will not be met with his condemnation. I know he will give His body to His followers..."

"Thank you, my Ethiopian friend," the centurion replied, wiping the perspiration dripping like hail from his face. "But will you tell me where I can learn in detail more about the Crucified One and what the phrase 'the Son of God' means — words which involuntarily escaped my tongue? And what were those miracles I witnessed today?"

Arraim looked at him thoughtfully.

"Do not lose sight of this disciple," he answered, pointing to John. "He will tell you everything and you will learn Who the Crucified One was."

"And you will be the first crucified Christian," added he in whisper, addressing me. "Let us leave this place, Argive," he said aloud, "let there be no extra eyes around while the Mother is pouring forth her grief..."

We started slowly down the hill. Here and there lay people who still had not come to their senses from their shock of mortal horror. Several houses had collapsed from the quake. The sky had cleared a little, but the night was already stretching its veil over the land, which was still shaking from time to time. In the distance appeared a handful of people in a hurry, among whom I recognized the wise Joseph of Arimathea by his long white beard.

The penultimate chord of the Great Cosmic Mystery had ended. Then the final one began — the Greatest.

Peace be with you, Empedocles!

**Thales of Argos**

# VIII. The Resurrection of Christ

*Thales of Argos to Empedocles,*
*the son of Miles of Athens —*
*at the infinite power of*
*the Crucified Love — rejoice!*

THE EVENING of the third day after the Ineffable Sacrifice was approaching. Yet the evening twilight had still not brought its multicoloured glints to the vault of the sky. Meanwhile I, Thales of Argos, in the Garden of Gethsemane, near the stone that seemed not to have yet dried up from the Divine tears, was praying to the One Ra. And for the first time on the planet Earth, the Great Initiate attached the Name of the Crucified God to the Name of his Mother.

And no sooner had this Name escaped my lips — lips that had uttered the words of a secret prayer in the sacred language of our ancestors — than from the heights of the Cosmos, as a distant response, choirs of bright evolution echoed to me, Thales of Argos, and their wings began to flutter around me in joyful astonishment:

"Blessed are you, O noble wise man, who has been the first to cast the new Name of God into the infinite depths of the Cosmos," whispered their fleshless lips.

"Glory to Thales of Argos, glory!" roared the spirits of the element of air. "Glory to him who has summoned the new Name of the One and Only!"

And I, Thales of Argos, heard the quiet joyful sigh of Mother Earth.

"Accept my blessing, my son, great and wise child of mine," whispered the Earth, "for the new Name of the One God has been uttered by you as a human being, my flesh and my heart! Mother Earth thanks you, my wise son Argive!"

And again I pronounced glorification to God the Pantocrator, the Crucified Christ, and then all Nature — including the vales and the heights of the Earth, and the firmament — repeated my words in a quiet whisper. And my chest was overflowing with great power, as if all the might of the Divine Cosmos had been gathered therein.

"Truly brave and wise you are, Argive," the words of Arraim the Four-time Greatest, reverberated behind my back, "that you have dared, before the Ineffable Sacrament, to pronounce the new Name of the One Lord!"

"Oh, no, it was not earlier, O Four-time Greatest," I answered, "for this Sacrament had already occurred within my heart, and my faith is the great altar which will support the entire Universe!"

Arraim looked intently at me.

"Truly," he replied, "Hellas is blessed thanks to you, O Sage, and among the four human evolutions that I, Arraim, observed on my wanderings across the fields of the Most High, there has never been anyone wiser and braver than you! But," he continued, putting his hand on my shoulder, "is it not time for us, Argive, to go to the place where the Divine Body rests?"

I, Thales of Argos, expected this invitation and, after silently nodding my head, slowly followed Arraim. He came out of the garden, went into the city and there, after entering one of the little houses, returned, holding the hand of the young disciple of the Crucified One — gentle John.

Upon seeing me, he fell on my shoulder and wept for a long time, painfully and grievously.

"Do you really not believe, John?" I, Thales of Argos, seriously asked and both my breath and my power fell on the head of the young disciple.

"Oh, you are wrong, O wise foreigner," John replied to me, "my faith is indestructible, yet I am just an ordinary human being, and is the human heart able to endure the grief of these past days?"

"You are not that ordinary a human being, John," I said and, after tilting my shoulders back slightly, my gaze peered piercingly into his eyes. "Remember, John, I adjure you, remember the Lemurian Sea and the Land of the Dragon! Remember, John, our meeting at the throne of Queen Balqis! Remember your name, O son of Atlantis!"

And the eyes of the young man opened wide, and they suddenly blazed up with the Fire of the Great Cognition.

"I am Lao-Tzu, the son of the Land of the Dragon!" he whispered. "And I... I knew that He — my God and my Saviour — will call me unto Himself!"

Meanwhile, someone was coming to us from behind — someone gentle, endearing, and quiet. This was She, the Mother of all Creation, the Eternally Young Virgin-Mother, Primordial Isis, the Heavenly Queen, the Blessed Virgin Mary. All three — I, Thales of Argos, Arraim the Four-time Greatest, and the disciple John — fell into the dust before Her.

"Stand up, my wise servants — you, Arraim, and you, Argive," rang out her voice above us. "And you, too, my son John, stand up to lead your Mother to where the last Will of the Supreme is to be carried out. Let us go, O Sages, for your Wisdom long ago ceased to be human wisdom, and to its eyes will be revealed that which the eyes of the sons of the Earth are still unable to see..."

"And you, Argive," She addressed me, "you who have interwoven your thread with Divine threads, for who else but you transmitted to me, your Egyptian Mother, the impulse that defeated the flesh of my eyes, and who else but you have awakened the memory of my son John and revealed Cosmic depths to him? You, Argive, I say, be my second son; and you, my eternally faithful servant and the King of my black children, all-wise Arraim, be my third son. And so, stand up, Love, Wisdom, and Power — my children, my sons, and let us come to greet the Victor, my Son in the flesh and my Father in the Spirit!"

The evening Aurora had already flooded the vault of the sky with the blood of her virgin cheeks, when the four of us entered into the extensive garden of Joseph of Arimathea. We disappeared under the shadow of cedars that surrounded the rock, on the opposite slope of which was a grotto guarded by a dozen Roman soldiers.

"Hold back your eyes, Sages," She — the Mother of the Crucified God — told us authoritatively, "for it does not befit you to see the secret bowels of my Son's sepulchre. But you, Arraim, harness your will and summon here the three Marys — three loving hearts — and let them find here the reward for their love and loyalty!"

Then powerful magic words resounded commandingly, whose power emanated from the darkened eyes of the Four-time Greatest One and spread like a sheaf of lightning bolts. In less than half an hour, in the distance there appeared three female figures hurrying along the dusty road. The first was Mary Magdalene; the second was that strange Jewish girl from under whose veil the eyes of Pallas Athena once peered at me; and the third was the mother of the sons of Zebedee, a gentle woman, a loving, obedient, and quiet mother, great in her love and humility — the maternal aspect that had not spared the sons' flesh to serve the Divine Sacrifice. The Magdalene ran up to the Mother of my Lord, and fell on her knees.

"O Mother!" she uttered, bursting into tears, "we don't know what happened to us, but we heard your voice and don't understand ourselves how we happened to come running here..."

"It was necessary," said the Virgin Mary quietly. "You shall stay with me here in prayer until the midnight hour..."

And after tenderly nodding to me and Arraim, She went with the women and John into a thicket of trees to pray.

"Come Argive, let us record on the scroll of our memory the coming Sacrament," Arraim proposed. "For the time is already drawing near..."

"O! My Lord!" Arraim suddenly sighed deeply, prostrating himself.

And I, Thales of Argos, against the background of a crimson sky, beheld a marvellous, unforgettable picture: two giant eyes, each with wings, occupying one fourth of the firmament. These wondrous winged eyes, with their indescribable power of anxious, passionate anticipation, were motionlessly gazing at the rock concealing the sepulchre of the Crucified One. And above the eyes was rising a forehead crowned with golden hair — those strands of hair being the stellar threads of the whole Cosmos, the entire Universe, cascading into the infinite depths of Creation. The lips were like a seven-stringed sistrum, sounding with eternal praise to the One Creator.

And I, Thales of Argos, saw that there were no barriers for the enormous eyes. They were peering into the very depths of the rock, observing therein something both miraculous and terrible, for the sake of which it was worth waiting for myriads of declining eternities. And this Sacrament, within the bowels of the rock, contained something whose accomplishment the wondrous owner of the gigantic winged eyes passionately wanted with all His being, clothed in the worlds of the Universe.

And I, Thales of Argos, realized that my strange destiny had given me the inexpressible moment of beholding the Demiurge Himself, the Sweetest Radiant One, the All-bright Morning Star, the Firstborn Son of the Hypostasis of the Original Triad.

"O Primordial Light, the Awakened Day, the First-born Child of Creation, the Father of the Element of Fire, accept my veneration!" I, Thales of Argos, exclaimed with fullness of heart, being unable to avert my gaze from the wondrous eyes in whose depths I beheld the homeland of human souls, including my own cradle.

And then behind the powerful head of the Demiurge, there seemed to blaze up a great light, and in that light there started to swarm innumerable cohorts of superhuman evolution. And this light, this resplendent path, stretched into such depths of Infinity as had never dawned even as a thought, even upon the reasoning of the Great Initiate. There was no end to this ribbon — the rainbow of Creation, glistening with all the colours of the Solar World. And I, Thales of Argos, realized that the end of this rainbow was to be found only at the Throne of the Ineffable One...

And I, Thales of Argos, saw two creatures of heavenly beauty standing beside Arraim the Four-time Greatest, who was prostrating himself in the dust. And with wings behind their backs — black with blue stripes — they bent over Arraim and tenderly whispered something in his ear. And I, Thales of Argos, was able to understand that these beings were the sons of the true race of Arraim. He stood up, and his first glance in my direction was full of amazement.

"What?!" he exclaimed. "You, a human being, have seen the Light-bearing One and yet you still conceal a Ray of Life within your body?"

And I, Thales of Argos, a human being indeed, a son of the dust of Mother Earth, straightened up and proudly replied to Arraim:

"What could the Light-bearing Demiurge do to me, Thales of Argos, a human being and a son of the Earth, if I was sitting in full consciousness at the right hand of God Himself in the garden of Magdala?!"

And the Four-time Greatest bowed low before me.

"Truly," he whispered, "the Earth in your person, O wise Argive, has defeated the Cosmos by the power of the One God... It is not me who will lead you, Argive," he continued, "but I ask *you* to lead me further, to where we are to behold the Awakened One..."

And I, Thales of Argos, boldly went forward. And all around — even though the night had already come — nothing was sleeping, but everything seemed to be lying in wait, anticipating the completion of the Sacrament of the great victory of the Spirit over the Flesh within its bowels.

In front of the sealed cave Roman soldiers were sleeping. They did not notice how subtle rays of golden light were already pouring forth through the crevices of the stone leaning against the sepulchre.

The silence around was indescribable. And the winged eyes were still burning in the firmament, while multitudes of beings of supreme evolution were still stretching heavenwards like a rainbow road, and the spirits of the elemental forces, gathering around, were singing hymns of endless harmonies with their inaudible voices.

And in the silence just one sound reverberated — high, pure, and gentle; it reverberated and fell silent. But then it arose again — yet even purer, even gentler... And suddenly, like brothers and sisters, sounds rolled forth in waves. However, these were not solemn sounds, as you might think, Empedocles, but sounds of gentle and quiet glorification. It was not a victorious or triumphant hymn, but the loving return of the Crucified God to the same human flesh that had crucified Him. It was not a triumph that sounded but All-forgiveness, for what kind of a victory could possibly belong to the Almighty and Omnipotent Lord?

And after turning slowly and quietly, the leaning stone fell, and a bright light gushed like a wave from the sepulchre, and at its threshold appeared the wondrous figure of Jesus Christ.

Bright and blissful was His Divine Countenance. His gentle eyes were shining with endless Love, and His first glance was to where the winged eyes of the Demiurge were burning in the vault of Heaven — eyes which at once flared up with Divine rapture. And the lips of the Light-bearing One opened, and a hymn of inexpressible solemnity poured forth from them, bringing into the depths of Chaos the construction of new worlds based on the new principles of victory over death...

Raising His right hand, Christ stretched it out in the direction of the Radiant One, and then above the brow of the Light-Bearer blazed up a symbol of the Primordial Union with the Light of Divine Love — a cross entwined with blood-red flowers of the Divine Sacrifice.

And the hymn of the Demiurge was caught up by the multitudes of beings in both superhuman and elemental evolution and, behold, the entire Universe was singing, the whole Cosmos, and even the bass notes, upon awakening, responded from the abyss of Chaos.

And again the right hand of the Awakened Lord arose, ever blessing. And He said quietly:

"Enough, children! Go to your homes. Leave Me alone for the time being with the poor children of the Earth, now regained for My Kingdom."

And the choruses fell silent, and the hymns spread abroad, the winged eyes faded away, and the cohorts of superhuman and elemental evolution became pale. And lo — before the face of the Earth and humanity again appeared the meek carpenter Jesus, who had conquered death by the power of His God-humanhood.

And the Earth responded: the first sound was the sound of terror produced by the group of Roman soldiers who were awakened and blinded by the light. And I watched as the lonely figure of a woman rushed first to the opened tomb, and she ran quickly to follow after Christ, who was slowly moving along the road. I recognized her: it was Mary Magdalene.

"O Lord..." she was about to start, but then, upon looking more attentively, she rushed to the feet of the Awakened One with a cry of joyful fright.

"Do not touch Me, Mary," the Lord softly told her, "for I am still full of Heavenly Glory and it will burn you down... Stand up and go warn My disciples, let them wait for Me in Galilee, under our cedars... Arise, Human Love, now transformed into Divine Love, arise, gentle Mary, the Mother of all the future Marys manifest in the flesh!"

And after blessing the weeping Mary, the Lord moved slowly on, where His Mother was waiting along with two other women. However, on His way to them, He also met us: Arraim the Four-time Greatest and me, Thales of Argos, a child of the Earth.

Meekly and tenderly, the awakened carpenter and Vigilant God was looking at us.

"Argive!" His gentle voice resounded. "I untie your bonds with humanity and bless you for a new Service. But first, you need to complete your great task on the Earth. I entrust to you, son of the Earth, a particle of My Power," and His hand touched my brow. "Take it to the distant caves of Ethiopia and give new life to the Primordial Queen of the Earth's dust, creeping on the ground, and also bring thereto My beloved daughter. Let her stay there with the daughter of Arraim, My servant, until I tell her to rise and serve Me..."

And I, Thales of Argos, watched as the Mother of my Lord brought closer to Him that humble Judean girl, from under whose veil the eyes of Pallas Athena once glanced at me.

"Here she is, My daughter," my Lord said to me, "manifest for the coming ages under the name of Sophia, the Supreme Wisdom of God. I entrust her to you, Argive, and she in turn will bring to the suffering Balqis everything that you earlier predicted for her, O wise Hellene, driven by My Spirit. Accept My blessing, Argive, and do not hesitate. Leave Me here for a while with My Mother, along with the third Mary and My servant Arraim. Embark, My Hellene, on a marvellous and faraway journey of your blessed life!"

And I, Thales of Argos, after prostrating myself at the feet of my Lord, took the hand of the silent girl and, without turning — for I was on God's path — went out of Joseph of Arimathea's garden.

We had just come out of the garden when we saw a man coming towards us with a long white beard; he was leading on a leash two white camels, who looked all ready to embark on a journey. At the moment of our meeting, he bowed low before me and said:

"Will the noble and wise Thales of Argos permit his old friend to serve him again with camels for his long journey with his sacred travelling companion?"

"Your feet are also the Lord's path, Rabbi Israel from Ur of the Chaldees," I responded. "On behalf of my companion I thank you, O Sage."

I did not talk any more with Rabbi Israel, for what was there in matter that could be hidden from the gaze of the old Chaldean?

Days and nights my veiled companion was silent, until far away in the distance the familiar outlines of the Ethiopian mountains began to shine.

In the depths of the mountain temple of the Goddess Ishtar, I found the secret place of residence of Queen Balqis. She had left the throne long ago, and had exchanged the royal crown for the veil of the senior priestess of the cloistered female Sanctuary.

After leaving my companion in the outer courtyard of the temple, I entered alone into the chamber of the beautiful Balqis.

She was sitting bent over a pile of ancient parchment scrolls. This was still the same wonderfully, indescribably beautiful woman — only the wrinkles of deep suffering and age-long reflection had left their mark on her high forehead.

With her first glance at me, a deep cry escaped from her exquisite lips:

"O wise Hellene!"

And then I, Thales of Argos, beheld the proud Queen of Sheba, the beautiful Balqis, the daughter of Arraim the Four-time Greatest, lying in the dust at my feet.

I did not lift her, for on my lips there were no speeches or messages of my own, but only those of the Divine Sufferer.

Only after telling her everything, did I allow Balqis to stand up, and I saw her countenance renewed by the streams of sweet tears and revived by Divine Love.

"Weak Balqis has no words to express gratitude to you, O Divine ambassador," she said. "And do you really need it? But where is your mysterious travelling companion, whom I need to protect according to the words of the Greatest of the Greatest?"

And then when I brought the Holy Sophia into Balqis' chamber — the Queen shot up at the sight of her open face and stretched forth her hands in unspeakable horror.

"Arra! Arra!" she said indistinctly, and again fell into dust before the new arrival.

And for the first time I heard the voice of the Divine Sophia. And this voice was like a combination of billions of other voices risen from the depths of the Cosmos, and it was similar to the crying of sistrums of all the temples of the Mother Goddess, more sonorous than angelic choirs:

"I am not Arra, my sister, O beautiful Balqis. I am the mother of all the Arras of the whole Universe, for all Arras since the beginning of time have been born in my uncreated heart," she said, and her hand endearingly rested upon Balqis' black braids. "Stand up, my sister, O wise Balqis, stand up and accept me under your mysterious shelter until the voice of my Lord and Father summons me into the world.

"And you, thrice blessed Hellene," the Divine Sophia addressed me, "accept from me as well a blessing — both for your new path and for the end of your human path..."

And I, Thales of Argos, after prostrating myself at the feet of the New Mystery of the Cosmos, came out of the temple and continued my journey to the Primordial Queen of the Earth's dust.

For six days I, Thales of Argos, walked through underground passages and river channels in the bowels of the Earth, fearlessly crossing earthly chasms and crawling through the narrow corridors and crevices of pristine granite boulders. And the Beacon of Eternity ignited by me above my forehead illumined my way, and my guide was the Great Wisdom of the Theban Sanctuary.

Finally I reached a layer of ruby rocks and there, in a chamber hollowed out of an entire giant emerald, I found her — the marvellous Queen of Serpents, who so faithfully served my Wisdom on the day of my first visit to Queen Balqis. And the wondrous Serpent straightened up, standing on the end of her tail, and fixed her ruby eyes on me: myriads of years of agonizing waiting shone in her gaze.

And I, Thales of Argos, bravely raised my hand, and after imperiously summoning the new Name of One God, by the particle of His Power given to me, I commanded for a Great Being to rise from the depths of non-existence — the Primordial King of the Earth's dust, the progenitor of the human race, the wondrous creation of the Builders' Wisdom.

In obedience to my imperious call, he arose, the Firstborn Adam, in all his marvellous and indescribable beauty, gentle and loving, he arose in all the angelic pristine innocence of his paradise existence.

And I, Thales of Argos, touched the forehead of the Queen of Serpents, and said:

"By the will of our Lord Jesus Christ, Who came in the flesh to save sinners of the whole world since the day of Creation, I command you, O all-wise Lilith, to leave the image of Wisdom creeping upon the Earth, to assume again your pristine image, and to join your spouse!"

It was as though a thousand thunders had scattered across the ruby cave — the snake skin fell off. And in front of me, Thales of Argos, there appeared in all her inexpressible beauty and power the Primordial Lilith, bright and joyful, for she received what she had not had since her creation — a particle of Divine Love. And the Primordial Adam opened wide his embraces towards her, and they merged together, and in the astral waves of harmony, they disappeared in the depths of the World of Cosmic Schemes and Designs.

And then I, Thales of Argos, raised a prayer of gratitude to the Lord Jesus Christ and by the power of my Wisdom I transferred my body from the bowels of the Earth to the desert of Arabia, where my new path was about to begin.

I call upon the blessing of the gentle Galilean carpenter — the Supreme God — to descend upon you, my friend Empedocles!

Amen.

**Thales of Argos**

# The Unfinished Chapter

IN THE MANUSCRIPTS of Anastasia Theodoridi has been preserved a small fragment of an unfinished chapter that reflects the conversation of Thales of Argos with the King and Father of our planet in the Temple of Silence before the arrival of the Resurrected Christ.

Melchizedek tells Argive: "My son! I knew that His Love is boundless, yet I realized the entire grandeur of the Divine Sacrifice only in those minutes when, after enduring His great sufferings, the God was meekly walking to Calvary. It was not death that was terrible. He could not die. But what was terrible was that great abyss of sufferings which opened wide over us. We saw how at the moment of His Resurrection a whole chain of new calvaries was unfolding in its endlessness. For the first time we were horrified at the Great Sacrifice of Love that He has brought to us, the Leaders of Humanity. While we have gone through the whole lesson given to us at the dawn of creation, our work has seemed to us so miserable and pathetic, compared to what His Divine Love has accomplished."

And further, from the lips of Melchizedek resonated repentance for the futility of any, even the highest, earthly glory before Christ's Crown of Thorns. Then the Fourth Initiation was to follow, when candidates gathered at the Temple of Silence to be present at the last meeting with the Risen One: "Before His Ascension, He will come to us and bring us the New Covenant with the One and Only, for everything that we have done is finished."

Thales of Argos, in anticipation of the appearance of Christ, relieves the tension of his will, for he has realized that he has no will, and all this time he has been fulfilling the will of the Resurrected One. Together with other Initiates he has to "enter the cosmic life, and what human will means there..."

This unfinished chapter breaks off at the lines when the Great Beacons have entered the Temple before the arrival of the World Teacher.

# Letter to Readers

I, THALES OF ARGOS, know that your child-like souls yearn for fairy tales, yearn for eternal truths enclothed in immortal images, which tell in your world of a language known to all — a language spoken in the land where golden branches are reflected in the waters of Life. This is the language which each of you once spoke and which your child-like soul remembers with love, longing for its exquisite fragrance. And, although many of you outgrew fairy tales long ago, those who are thirsty for knowledge remain forever like happy children who sit and eagerly listen, aspiring to knowledge and beauty. They always feel they are awakening inside, no matter how many times they hear those stories, to constantly repeat them, just as they once did in their childhood: "tell it one more time," "tell it again," "tell it once again... and?... and?... and?..."

This is the language that you, the people of the last century of this millennium, started to forget, being interested only in studying the language of technology and materialistic sciences, while the language of Truth has been turned into a mummy. However, you need to apply efforts to learn it again, now in a new form, as the language of the heart and of your consciousness, which is now awakening and developing within you — the language of spiritual science.

Therefore, as an initial impulse, linking the old with the new, in the years of the great battle that flooded the Eastern lands with blood and was approaching your country, I sent my messenger in the appearance of a silent monk into the city of Galați which the Gauls erected on your lands on the shores of the Danube, or the Istros, to bring these letters to you, as once *Varlaam and Ioasaf* were. They were then to be translated into your tongue and brought to Tomis, the entry gates for the wisdom of Hellas into your lands, and from thence, through the disciple of Asclepius — the son of Apollo and a doctor — and further delivered to all of you.

I know that some of you have copied them by your own hand and read them every year, one by one, during Holy Week, every evening. At the same time, others have grown so fond of them that they came to believe that they themselves had written them — and this is well and good. For any truth that becomes in us a source of truth is ours — it belongs to all of us equally.

And Empedocles, at the beginning of the present epoch, the seeker of the "I," returned to you in the image of Faustus — in fact, each and every one of you are him, the people of this pivotal century, who fight with the two faces of evil. You strive to reach your true Self and to act from the eternal, invariable Core of Existence, so as to come again in a new image, being completely free, to the realm where golden branches are reflected in the waters of life and where the living language understood by all is spoken — the language of future understanding between people and Gods — the language of the Spiritual Epoch.

With the blessing of the redeeming Divine Love, the Sacred Wisdom of humanity, and Saint Sophia, who heralds the Great Revelation for the end of our millennium, may all those who read it rejoice!

**Thales of Argos**

# *Afterword*

**T**HE FOREWORD by Zinovya Dushkova evokes a sense of incompleteness. But this is why it has been said that the final full stop has not been put and that the Afterword is still ahead.

Once the Lords of Karma trace in the Akashic Records the progress of *The Mystery of Christ* in the minds and hearts of readers — and, most importantly, all those who are mentioned therein — Zinovya Dushkova may give the Afterword dedicated to the Mystery of Christ — the Mystery of Sophia, which is unfolding in the present time. This text is planned to be published in the form of a book that might see the light in the coming years. And then after the publication of this book, chances are good that the third part of the Records will be released, which together with *The Mystery of Christ* will compose a trilogy.

Therefore, if *The Mystery of Christ* by Thales of Argos has struck a chord in your heart and you would like to be among the first to know when the Afterword appears, which casts light on some currently living characters, then subscribe to the newsletter of Zinovya Dushkova's website here:

www.dushkova.com/en/thales

In the meantime, you might draw your attention to Zinovya Dushkova's book *The Great Initiate*, which was narrated on New Year's Eve in 2016 and recorded amidst the snow-covered peaks of the Himalayas. It will immerse you in spheres where past, present, and future times criss-cross, revealing some of the secret pages from the life of Thales of Argos, whose destiny is inseparably linked with that of Arra — the New Mystery of the Cosmos.

And if you are wondering what is that Great Revelation destined to appear at the end of the last millennium, which Thales of Argos spoke of in his letter — this is *The Teaching of the Heart*. It is a series of thirteen books written by Zinovya Dushkova in 1997–1998, and first published in English between 2016 and 2020. The appearance of *The Teaching of the Heart* in Russia at the end of the 20th century was predicted by such famous seers as Mitar Tarabich,[1] Edgar Cayce,[2] and Vanga,[3] as well as Helena Roerich.[4]

Finally, if you have enjoyed *The Mystery of Christ*, you can help other people discover this book by writing a review or just leaving a rating wherever you bought it. This might take only a few minutes, yet it will make a huge difference in bringing this work to the attention of other readers.

Thank you so much!

**The Publisher**

# *Glossary*

**Adonai** (*Hebrew*, "my Lord") — one of the names of God in Judaism.

**Akasha** (*Sanskrit*, "sky") — Primeval Matter, also known as *Materia Matrix*; the refined, supersensible spiritual essence which pervades all space; primary cosmic substance.

The Akashic Records are a particular manifestation of the limitless and indestructible memory of Nature, which stores information about all events and manifestations of the Cosmos — people, planet, system, or anything else.

**Apocryphal** (*Greek*, "hidden away") — sacred and secret. *Apocrypha* denotes hidden or secret writings.

**Argive** (*Greek*) — a native of the city of Argos in Greece.

**Atlantis** (*Greek*) — Plato's name for the continent whereon the Fourth Race of humanity developed. Extending from the North to the South, it was located in an area now covered by the waters of the Atlantic Ocean.

Numerous islands rose from the depths to form this continent, beginning some five million years ago. At the same time, the Great Teachers started gathering and resettling on one of the central islands the best representatives of the Third Race from the continent of Lemuria, whose time was drawing to a close.

The first Atlanteans were almost three-and-a-half metres tall, later decreasing in height to approximately two-and-a-half metres. The peak of Atlantis' flourishing coincided with the Toltec period, when, after long internecine wars, tribes united into a federation headed by an emperor. The capital was the City of Golden Gates.

The Great Teachers living among the people had imparted to the Atlanteans an abundance of mystic knowledge, enabling them to achieve success in many spheres of life — they were able to manage the most powerful energies; they knew the mysteries of Nature and could breed new species of plants and animals; they could come up with the most complex technologies, including the science of aeronautics; in addition, they made direct contact with the Distant Worlds.

The decline of Atlantis began with the fall of Lucifer, who had been one of humanity's trusted Instructors. People began to use mystic knowledge not for the good of all but for glorifying themselves, accumulating riches, inventing deadly weapons, waging war, practising dark magic, and so on. Those who warned of the inevitable disaster resulting from the actions of the Atlanteans faced a death penalty. This frightful moral decline, along with the humiliation of women and other perversions, led to the Atlanteans consciously repeating the sins of primitive people, the progenitors of the primary apes; the sexual intercourse between some Atlanteans and primary apes produced man-like monkeys.

The violation of Cosmic Laws on such an unprecedented scale, along with the use of dark magic by the Atlanteans against the Sons of Light, brought destructive elemental forces into play. These gradually destroyed Atlantis and ushered in the Ice Age, covering whole regions of the planet with ice.

The main continent was destroyed by water a few millions years ago, leaving a number of large and small islands, among which were Ruta and Daitya. The isle of Ruta sank almost 850,000 years ago, and Daitya submerged nearly 270,000 years ago, leaving a smaller island known as Poseidonis.

Prior to these disasters, the Sons of Light resettled the best and most spiritual inhabitants of Atlantis to

Egypt, transferring there the entire mystic heritage of the Atlanteans. The Masters themselves moved to Shambhala, which was also an island at the time. They have been helping humanity secretly ever since, without revealing themselves.

Today, Atlantis is slowly rising and will be the continent for the development of the Sixth and Seventh Races of humanity.

**Baphomet** (*Greek*) — one of the names of the Lord of the Underground Fire. Many have portrayed him as an idol, but Helena Blavatsky said that this word has never meant "goat," either esoterically or philologically, nor even anything so objective as an idol. He can be attributed to the astral deity, who at the same time is also the bearer of the lowest Underground Fire. Besides, Baphomet serves as a kind of connecting link with the world of astral forms, through which one can pave the way to comprehending the higher spheres.

**Beacon of Eternity** — a special sign, invisible to the physical eyes, on the forehead of a person who has passed an Initiation. These signs of a particular colour, indicating a level of spirituality, are usually represented as a shining star, but may also take the form of a designated symbol.

**Bel** (*Chaldean*, "Lord") — the oldest and most powerful God of Babylonia.

**Brotherhood** — the Community of the Seven Messengers of the Distant Worlds and their disciples, who have lived side by side with humanity on the Earth for millions of years, developing the human mind and heart. This Brotherhood is usually called White to indicate the White Light that, upon splitting, yields the seven colours of the rainbow, each of which symbolizes one of the Great

Teachers; and vice versa — the seven colours of the rainbow result in the White Light after their fusion.

The previous Solar System was tasked with giving people knowledge and developing their intelligence. The present System is aimed at bringing people closer to Love, and the focus of Love is the Heart. Therefore, the Great Lords have divided themselves into two Lodges — the Western and the Eastern.

The Western Lodge — also known as the Brotherhood of Luxor or the Thebes Sanctuary, located in Egypt — was to provide knowledge, as well as to develop and expand people's consciousness, with emphasis on the mental body, the mind, the human intellect, in order to help to take a step towards the heart. All the knowledge accumulated in the past and present Solar Systems, resides exclusively in Egypt.

The Eastern Lodge — Shambhala or the Himalayan Brotherhood — was to develop the intuition of the heart, always bearing Love and serving the highest energies. In other words, the West is the mind, and the East is the heart. We learn from ancient traditions that the Masters left the West for the East. Many people, in fact, left the Sanctuary in Egypt to go to the East. This happens approximately once every two thousand years.

At the end of the 19th century, before the start of Armageddon, all the Secret Schools and Ashrams of the Western Brotherhood were closed and moved to the Himalayas. All the Great Teachers who had worked in the world — holding Initiations and imparting knowledge — were also summoned to the Stronghold of Light in the Himalayas. Humanity was abandoned for a hundred years, but knowledge was still given through their disciples. However, there was no longer any direct contact between the Masters and the vast majority of people.

The Theban Sanctuary is now re-opening and once again starting to serve Love. While previously it was working through the Ray of Knowledge, now these two Sanctuaries — the Eastern and the Western — are uniting and interpenetrating their Rays, imparting a Single Ray of Love-Wisdom. Similarly, all the Great Lords who had been saturating humanity as much as possible with knowledge are now beginning to serve Love. Thus a Great Synthesis is being born, and the two Greatest Schools are merging into one, affirming a single path for the whole world: the ascent to the steps of Wisdom through the illumination of the human heart.

**Cabeiri** (*Greek*) — ancient deities, who were said to possess a mysterious force capable of delivering both people and the areas of their dwelling from all troubles and dangers. Simultaneously, in the role of rescuers, certain "retributive" functions were attributed to them, because they meted out punishment for unflattering misdeeds.

The Cabeiri also included Titans who came from other planetary systems, many of whom, after staying in the thick of unenlightened human masses, ascended to the level of Lords of Karma. They carry out their invisible Labour, weighing — on the Karmic Scales — those *causes* which have led either a person, a people, a country, or indeed a whole continent to certain *effects*. And each is rewarded or punished according to their fruits.

**Chaldeans** — a caste of learned Kabbalists in Babylonia, who could be savants, magicians, astrologers, or diviners.

**Chintamani** (*Sanskrit*, "magical jewel") — the Gift of the constellation of Orion to the planet Earth; the mystical Stone manifest as the Treasure of the World, which is destined to bring happiness and prosperity to all living beings.

Despite the fact that it has Twin Brothers, nevertheless, it is a crown-bearer, for it was created by a single impulse of the Universe at the dawn of Times. However, this Crown of Creation has its own prehistory, for the Spirit of the Stone was nurtured in the Heart of Infinity. And only the Gods of Sirius could see its Fire-breathing structure. They also brought the semi-rarefied Stone of Happiness into the constellation of Orion, thanks to which not only the star Betelgeuse acquired the status of a sacred celestial orb within a specific Cosmic Period. But here a division occurred and the Fiery Spirit of the Stone returned to Sirius, while its crystallized Light had been for a long time in the arms of Orion. Orion "nurtured" it by its own currents, literally bearing the Fruit that would embark on a journey to establish the Cosmic Balance in the depths of the Solar System — specifically, on the newborn planet Earth.

The Chintamani is preserved in the very heart of Shambhala, maintaining its link with fire-breathing cores of maternal stars, thanks to which the planet Earth still retains the orbit of her own revolution.

A fragment of the Chintamani can "travel" around the world, if the Seven Great Teachers take a unanimous decision to put it into the hands of their Messenger, who is destined to carry out Labour of cosmic significance. And then the fragment returns on its own and literally merges with the Treasure that has never left the boundaries of Shambhala.

Thus, in the 20th century, the fragment of the Chintamani was kept by the Roerich family, who received it in Paris on 6 October 1923.

**City of the Golden Gates** — the capital of Atlantis that was situated in the eastern part of the continent.

**Cyrene** (*Greek*) — an ancient Greek city consecrated to Apollo, which was on the territory of modern Libya.

**Dao** (*Chinese*, "way") — in Chinese philosophy, the perpetual action or the principle of creation, which is responsible for the origin of both oneness and duality, and at the same time for the beginning of the world and creation.

**Demiurge** (*Greek*, "Creator") — the Planetary Spirit, the Supreme Lord or Ruler of the planet Earth, who has passed His human evolution and reached an incredibly high level of spiritual development. Together with other High Spirits constituting the Hierarchy of Light, He is now responsible for the creation, preservation, and transfiguration of the Earth.

The Planetary Spirit is androgynous, because on the higher planes of Existence there is no gender separation — hence, the pronoun *He* is used merely for lack of a more appropriate one. The Planetary Spirit is able to manifest Himself in various Aspects and Hypostases, including male and female in the binary world, since He bears within Himself both Principles.

As a rule, the governing Hierarchy of Light for young planets, such as the Earth, consists of High Spirits that came from Distant Worlds, wherein they long ago had gone through the given planet's stage of Evolution. When the humankind of such a planet reaches spiritual maturity, the Lords of Light who arrived from other Worlds leave it, to be replaced by worthy High Spirits who have already gone through their evolution on that young planet.

From ancient sacred texts, it is evident that the Planetary Spirit of the Earth is the Lord of Sirius. Besides, even the Quran states that Allah is the Lord of Sirius. However, it should be borne in mind that the God described in the Old Testament is not the Supreme Lord of the Earth whom Christ calls His Father in the New Testament.

Sometimes He whom we denote by the Name of *the One and Only* forms simultaneously several of His own Hypostases, as well as Individualities (under different names), and one that possesses a higher energy component serves for another (it may even be said, for Himself) as a Master, Teacher, and Protector — either in the physical world or in the Ethereal, depending on the single Goal which is set before His "emanating forms."

The Nativity Mystery of the Stellar Spirit of Sirius in the Glorious Body on the Higher Planes of the Earth occurred for the first time on the planet on 19 July 2017. It is of great significance not only for the Earth and the Solar System, but also for all the constellations headed and supervised by Sirius. This Mystery of Light will never be repeated in the present Grand Cycle of Evolution.

**Distant Cape** — the ancient name of the Cape of Good Hope; the land of the Distant Cape is the land of South Africa.

In *The Mystery of Christ* are mentioned twelve black slaves who carried the sedan-chair in which sat the wise Initiate of the Lunar Sanctuary — a grey-haired, strong Chaldean. Twelve is the number that has been followed since ancient times by those who have comprehended the mysteries of Nature, bringing closer to themselves different people, from disciples to ordinary slaves, regardless of their skin colour.

The Lunar Sanctuary dealt mainly with the "native" offspring of the Earth, observing and helping its wards in the transformation of the matter that constituted their quaternaries. And it is no coincidence that these slaves were from the land of the Distant Cape, which in ancient times was also called the Cape of Storms. Besides, it was associated with the cape which brought death, for a huge number of ships and sailors were buried in that zone. At one time it was the Point of Death, and not everyone who directed themselves towards India could sail by it safe and sound. But they were already endowing it with faith and hope for a successful outcome, turning to the Forces of Life. Of course, these were not random people.

Here the brave Phœnician Hanno might be mentioned, along with the distant voyages which he undertook in his past incarnations, dying more than once. Yet nevertheless, thanks to the strength of his spirit, he overcame this point of peril. This achievement later gave him the right to cross through the Gates of the Theban Sanctuary.

Of course, a special meaning is seen in the fact that the Sanctuary of Thebes sent its Initiate, Thales of Argos, to accompany Hanno on his distant expedition, which took place in the 5th century BCE. And then in the 15th century CE, it took the Portuguese a little over 40 years to cover the same route that Hanno had visited.

One of the farthest points of Hanno's journey was the island on which he discovered anthropoid apes. This island was also supposed to be under the jurisdiction of the Lunar Sanctuary, from where the Chaldeans took slaves. The island's territory was covered with a dark energy net, set by the Death Point of the Distant Cape. And it should be said that its destructive currents spread mainly along the west coast of Africa. On the island, its own experiments were carried out, since those apes were the "offspring" of those Atlanteans who "fell into sin" during the time of Atlantis, having intercourse with the largest species of the Animal Kingdom. Of course, the approaches to the giant Point of Death can be specked with "small satellites" that carry within themselves a destructive formula. The role of these satellites can be played by both certain areas and the people themselves that inhabit them, although most often the latter can be called "demi-human."

Hanno founded several cities on the path of his advancement, where he established temples — in other words, he laid the foundations of the Points of Life. And in all this he was assisted by Thales of Argos, who unmistakably indicated the areas destined for transformation — that is, for the "remelting" of the currents bringing death into the very energies which affirm Life. Of course, Thales of Argos was carrying out his invisible Labour in accord with the instruction of the Head of the Theban Sanctuary.

Hence, one of the final goals of Thales of Argos was a visit to the Distant Cape, where he performed a Labour of Hierarchically large dimensions: he neutralized the Point of Death, where, following the Cosmic Right, he pacified the elemental forces that ruled on the Cape of Storms by 50%, placing on it all his Hopes in the form of life-affirming fires, whose power has only increased over time, showing patronage to sailors up to the present day.

Thus, the Cape of Good Hope currently can also represent the arena of battle between the forces of evil and Good. Yet, nevertheless, it already serves as a focus of refraction of the rays coming from certain constellations, as well as from the planets of the Solar System, through which stellar "sendings" are periodically refracted.

**Distant Worlds** — the other planets in our Solar System, such as Venus, Jupiter, Uranus, and Pluto, as well as other star systems, for example, the constellations of Canis Major, Orion, Coma Berenices, and the Pleiades.

All planets and stars in the Universe are home to living beings, but they have varying degrees of tenuity in their matter structures. Therefore, people cannot see them either with the naked eye or with their telescopic devices, which are as yet far from perfect.

The Seven Great Teachers of Humanity, together with 144,000 High Spirits, who "follow the Lamb whithersoever He goeth," came to the Earth from the Distant Worlds to help humanity, most of them nearly eighteen million years ago. Gradually, they will leave the Earth, and their places will be taken by the Spirits, who have passed through their evolution on the Earth and attained the degree of Masters.

**Dravidians** (*Sanskrit*) — the oldest population of Hindustan.

**God** — the Divine, Unchangeable, Invariable, and Infinite Principle; the eternally Unknowable Cause of All that exists; omnipresent, all-pervading, visible and invisible spiritual Nature, which exists everywhere, in which everything lives, moves, and has its being; the Absolute, including the potential of all things as well as all universal manifestations. Upon being made manifest, out of its Absolute Oneness God becomes the Absolute of infinite differentiation and its consequences — relativity and opposites. God has no gender and cannot be imagined as a human being. In the Holy Scriptures, God is Fire, God is Love — the one primeval energy that conceives the worlds.

In cases when this word does not refer to the above, in ancient Teachings it has always meant the collectivity of the working and intelligent Forces in Nature. Thus, the world is ruled by the Creative Forces of the Cosmos, together constituting the limitless Hierarchy of Light, known as Jacob's Ladder in the Bible.

However, the Great Unknown was, is, and always will be hidden from the eyes of those who live in the manifest world. The Primal Cause, the Absolute, has been and will be unknowable — forever and ever.

The traditional Christian concept of *God* refers to the Planetary Spirit, or a *Demiurge*.

**Gods** — the Spirits of the Higher Spheres, Distant Worlds, who have succeeded in achieving a high level of evolution, far surpassing the level of earthly humanity that led to people beginning to perceive them as Gods. In other words, this level of spiritual achievement is destined for humanity as well.

In Tibet, such a Spirit is called by the ancient word *Lha* (*Tibetan*, "Spirit," "God"), which covers the entire series of celestial Hierarchies. Every Supreme Concept of the Cosmos is personified in a High Spirit, who takes a human form as well. That is why every ancient religion has a pantheon of Gods, each of whom, being an embodiment of a certain Idea, represents a particular Force of Nature.

The Sons of God, the Sons of Light, the Sons of Heaven, the Sons of Fire, the Sons of Reason, the Archangels, the Regents of Planets, the Masters of Wisdom, the Bodhisattvas (*Sanskrit*, "Enlightenment Beings"), the Dhyan Chohans (*Sanskrit*, "Lords of Light"), the Rishis (*Sanskrit*, "Sages of Insight"), the Kumaras (*Sanskrit*, "Youths"), and so on — these are High Spirits, who, like the Avatars, assumed a human appearance to raise the consciousness of humanity and accelerate its development. The Seven Great Spirits have taken care of the planet Earth and its humanity. Again and again, they were incarnated as the greatest founders of kingdoms, religions, sciences, and philosophies in order to help people unite with their Divine Nature. And so they have left deep traces in every domain of life and in every land. By the present time, each of them has educated disciples who have reached a high level of consciousness, and the number of the Leaders of Humanity is now 777.

For example, among their incarnations on the Earth are: Akbar the Great, Anaxagoras, Apollonius of Tyana, Confucius, the Count of Saint-Germain, Francis of Assisi, Gautama Buddha, Giordano Bruno, Hermes Trismegistus, Jakob Böhme, Jesus Christ, John the Apostle, Joseph, Joshua, King Arthur, Krishna, Lao-Tzu, Mahatma Koot Hoomi, Mahatma Morya, Melchizedek, Menes, Moses, Muhammad, Numa Pompilius, Origen, Orpheus, Paul the Apostle, Pericles, Plato, Pythagoras, Rama, Ramesses the Great, Sergius of Radonezh, Solomon, Thomas à Kempis, Thutmose III, Tsongkhapa, Tutankhamun, Zoroaster, and many others.

All the Gods have their Spouses, who in the Higher Worlds are united, and one does not exist without the other. But, since the Masculine Principle must express itself in the visible aspect of life and the Feminine Principle in the invisible, the Female Deities were revered as the most sacred and secret in all ancient religions. It is they — who have been incarnated on the Earth as mothers, sisters, daughters, and wives — through self-sacrifice, heroism, and continuous giving, inspired the Sons of Light and the peoples of the Earth, as well as humanity as a whole. Similarly, the entire Hierarchy of Light devoutly honours the Mother of the World — the Great Spirit of the Feminine Principle, who has Her personifications in many religions of the world as the Supreme Goddess. The Mother of the World incarnated Herself as Mary to give life to Jesus Christ. After that, for the past two thousand years, She has manifested Herself through Her

Hypostasis-Daughters — Faith, Hope, and Love, who have continuously replaced each other and have never abandoned this world.

**Grave-diggers of the Earth** — High Spirits, under whose supervision the Earth will be immersed in sleep during the period of *Pralaya*. Those who took upon themselves the role of Grave-diggers must not leave the Subtle Spheres of the Earth until the end of a certain Cycle of Evolution, even after their final earthly incarnation.

**Hellas** — the ancient name of Greece, which was inhabited by the Hellenes.

**Hierophant** (*Greek,* "one who explains sacred things") — a revealer of sacred knowledge and the Chief of the Initiates. A title belonging to the highest Adepts in the temples of antiquity, who were the teachers, expounders of the Mysteries, and the Initiated into the final great Mysteries. The Hierophant represented the Demiurge, and explained to the candidates for Initiation the various phenomena of Creation that were produced for their tuition.

**Horus** (*Egyptian,* "height," "sky") — the ancient Egyptian God of the Sky and the Sun, the son of Osiris and Isis.

The star of Horus is Sirius. Ancients also perceived Sirius as the Mother of Horus. In Greek legends the constellation of Canis Major was perceived as the Dog of Orion, while the Sumerians called it the "Dog of the Sun."

**Initiate** — one who has been entitled to acquire the Secret Knowledge of the Cosmos and human beings. Each new stage of Initiation reveals ever new mysteries and imparts new abilities.

Initiation ceremonies — or Mysteries — took place in Ancient Sanctuaries such as the Pyramids of Egypt, the

Temples of Greece and India, and so on. Secret Sanctuaries with halls for Initiations were built in places of powerful energy, mostly in the mountains. Mountains are the source of the strongest energy because their summits are covered with snow, which, like a natural lens, serves to receive the currents of other constellations and planets. Similarly, representatives of other worlds who study the Earth have their bases in the mountains, too.

The procedure of Initiation is a mystical penetration to a higher level of perception and comprehension of the mystery of Existence, thanks to the acceptance of higher-order currents and the ability to use them effectively. It is the transition from life to a temporary death by means of a magic dream, which in turn allows a candidate to experience a disembodied Spirit and Soul in the subjective world. Each Initiation requires moral purity, strength of spirit, and an aspiration towards Truth.

For example, Hermes Trismegistus (*Greek*, "Thrice-Greatest") underwent three Initiations, although he is already the Four-time-Greatest, having successfully passed through yet another. His father, Arraim, is a Four-time-Greatest as well. Thales of Argos passed through four Initiations. Christ passed through Eight Initiations, and His Second Coming is associated with His Ninth Initiation.

However, not only people and the Great Spirits may go through Initiations, but also realms of Nature, planets, stars, solar systems, etc. Thus, in the present day, humanity as a whole, also the Earth, are undergoing the next level of their Fiery Initiation.

**Ishtar** (*Chaldean*) — the Babylonian and Akkadian Goddess of Love and Beauty; the personification of the planet Venus.

**Isis** (*Egyptian*) — the ancient Egyptian Mother Goddess, the ideal of femininity and motherhood; personified Nature. The Christian image of God's Mother with the Child in her arms dates back to the image of Isis with the infant Horus.

**Jupiter** (*Latin*) — the ancient Roman God of Heaven, daylight, thunder; the Father of all the Gods; the Supreme Deity of the Romans, identified with the Greek Zeus.

**Kabbalah** (*Hebrew*, "tradition") — the ancient Chaldean Secret Doctrine and an occult system handed down by oral transmission. Once it was the fundamental science of cosmogony, but now has been distorted by centuries-old accretions and interpolations of western occultists, especially the Christian mystics.

The modern Kabbalah represents a mystic current in Judaism that emerged in the Middle Ages. It deals with esoteric interpretations of the Hebrew Scriptures and teaches several methods of interpreting Biblical allegories.

**Karma** (*Sanskrit*, "action") — the Cosmic Law of Cause and Effect, which is expressed in the formula, "as you sow, so shall you reap"; defines the frames within which the destiny of an individual, people, planet, and so on can be developed.

Karma neither punishes nor rewards, it is simply a single Universal Law that infallibly guides all other laws, producing certain effects in accordance with corresponding causes. Every word, action, thought, or desire leads to an appropriate effect — and, eventually, to everything in one's surroundings. Nothing happens accidentally. Karma may be not only individual but also collective, embracing whole peoples, continents, planets, and star systems. One cannot change or get rid of it except by eliminating the causes underlying the human actions.

Everyone bears the mark of karmic predestination right from birth. And their free will is limited by the frames determined by Karma, which is created by their own human will. However, the placing of obstacles and restrictions in one direction opens opportunities in another. The purpose of Karma is to direct everyone towards the path of Evolution. Hence Love is the quickest way of redeeming one's Karma.

**Kemet** (*Coptic*) — one of the names of Ancient Egypt.

**Land of Hor** — the area between two Mounts Hor in the Middle East. And although in *The Mystery of Christ* it is said that the Kingdom of Sheba, which was situated in the southern part of the Arabian Peninsula, was located "to the north of the land of Hor," it should be borne in mind that over the entire history of the Earth there have been frequent changes of the poles.

In the so-called Cretaceous period, this process was observed much less often, but over the past 10 million years, the pole change has occurred at least four times. And now the planet stands on the threshold of the yet another transformation of the North into the South and the South into the North. But on the scale of human life, it is difficult to track this process, since the complete change of the poles can take from one to several millennia.

Of course, the geological chronicle can preserve traces of past global processes, which are often associated with changes in geographical co-ordinates that are designated by the location of certain mountains and lands spread out between them, as well as the peoples inhabiting these areas. And the chronicle of the Human Race may have discrepancies in the recording of certain events or names, both due to certain "geopolitical" circumstances and in connection with the "human factor."

So, for example, Mount Hor initially represented a unified giant conglomerate. But then it started to undergo serious changes in its own configuration, dividing into two. It "drowned" its own gigantic foundation into the ground, leaving two peaks towering above the earthly surface. And now in present times, the space between them can be associated with the land of Hor.

As for the Titans of the North, they could have originally come from the South, completing their own cycle of evolution under the conditions of the North, as well as vice versa, since at the South Pole those had been "maturing" who were destined at the moment of the final change of the poles to appear in the form of the Titans of the North.

**Lemuria** — the name of the continent where the Third Race of humanity developed. It covered most of the present-day Pacific and Indian Oceans, stretching along the equator. Lemuria included today's Australia, New Zealand, Madagascar, and Easter Island.

Lemuria was the birthplace of physical humanity, since the first Races did not have matter bodies. The ethereal and sexless beings slowly began to take on density and, by the middle of the Third Race, people resembled beast-like giants, up to twenty metres tall. Even though their shapes were similar to animals, these were already human beings, though not yet rational. At the same time, a separation of the sexes of all creation gradually took place, and distinct male and female individuals appeared, along with certain animals of those times, i.e., dinosaurs. Being mindless, many male Lemurians had sexual intercourse with female animals and procreated a vicious breed of monsters — primeval apes. It was from these creatures that some Atlanteans — this time consciously — later engendered all currently existing species of man-like apes.

When humanity was ready to perceive knowledge, the Great Teachers came to the Earth from the Distant Worlds and endowed people with the Supreme Mind. This happened nearly eighteen million years ago.

The Great Teachers lived together with human beings. They cultivated morality in them through their examples, always being by their side as Elder Brothers. There was no need for religions in those days, since the Gods were right there with the people. The Messengers from the Distant Worlds had taught the Lemurians much in the way of science, providing them with the knowledge of highly developed planets. For example, they knew the properties of the Fire and fiery energies; they had knowledge of architecture, construction, mathematics, astronomy, agriculture, etc. Some of the plants — wheat, for instance — do not have wild-growing counterparts on the Earth, as they were the gifts of the Sons of Light from Venus. Likewise, bees and ants were brought from Venus for the edification of people: their diligence, along with their communal and hierarchical system, could serve as an example for humanity.

By the end of the Third Race, the Lemurians had achieved a highly developed civilization. Their physical bodies had become more perfect, and their height had been reduced to between six and seven-and-a-half metres; there was a similar evolution among animals, unusual species of which are still preserved in Australia. The Lemurians had built huge cities, and were impeccable masters of both arts and sciences. Humanity of that time can be compared with the civilization of the 19th century of the current era, but their knowledge of Nature and the Cosmos were far superior. Even so, those days saw the beginning of fierce confrontations between the Forces of the Light and the darkness.

When the Cosmic Period came for the next change of Races, the Great Teachers resettled the most spiritual and advanced representatives of Lemuria to new islands, which were soon to form a new Race on the new continent of Atlantis. Lemuria was destroyed by the Fire, that is, by extremely powerful earthquakes, and then submerged into the water about four million years ago.

Evidence of the existence of the Lemurians and their civilization has been preserved in the form of mysterious sculptures on Easter Island. And archæological excavations have also revealed huge skeletons which once belonged to the giants of that time.

**Lemurian Sea** — the Pacific Ocean, beneath whose waters now rests the continent of Lemuria.

**Lilith** (*Hebrew*) — as named in some apocryphal books, the wife of Lucifer. She is perceived as a demon, although the Bible does not mention this. Thus, in translation, according to Hebrew and Sumerian mythology, she is a "night being." Lilith represents the first woman fashioned from clay, who, according to Kabbalistic theory, was the first wife of Adam.

According to some more ancient texts, 144,000 Sons of Heaven descended, and a number of them entered into relationships with "women of the Earth," who differed little "intellectually" from representatives of the Animal Kingdom. But after the expiry of a certain period, the Sons of Life were destined to reunite with their "wives of Heaven," who now represented not "night" earthly beings, but "Solar" ones. And the latter, in contrast to the Lunar Lilith, were symbolically embodied in the biblical Eve.

**Lords of Karma** — the Spirits of the Universe, known as *Lipikas* (*Sanskrit*, "Scribes") in esoteric philosophy. These

Divine Beings are mystically connected with Karma, the Law of Retribution, for they are the Recorders, who impress on invisible tablets a "grand gallery of scenes of eternity" — i.e., a faithful record of every word, act, and even thought of everyone on the Earth, and of all that was, is, or ever will be in the manifest Universe. It is the Lords of Karma who project and make objective the ideal plan of the Universe, according to which the God-Creators re-create the Cosmos.

The Lipika Lords direct the evolution of the world, following Cosmic Laws and harmonizing their will with the evolution of the Cosmos. Against the will of the Lords of Karma human will is powerless, for the latter has created the former. To determine the course of human destiny, they use special matter that outlines the basis of the way which everyone must walk, being bound by karmic necessity.

However, the Lords of Destiny create precisely those conditions for humans, planets, systems, etc. that are necessary for the ascent along the Ladder of Evolution.

**Lunar Sanctuary** — a Sanctuary that united the native inhabitants of the Earth, who attained a certain level of knowledge about their maternal planet and the nature of elemental phenomena, thereby serving as the first enlighteners of unreasonable humanity.

By no means should such sanctuaries be confused with lunar temples, where orgies were held to please people's animal nature and newborn babies were sacrificed to "lunar gods."

Lunar Sanctuaries aimed to endow people with knowledge of the surrounding world and to contribute to the spiritualization of their ossified matter.

**Manvantara** (*Sanskrit*, "Age of a Manu") — a period of active life within a planet, system, galaxy, or the Universe. It is equivalent in duration to *Pralaya*.

**Melchizedek** (*Hebrew*, "king of righteousness") — one of the Hypostases of the Lord of Sirius manifested on the Earth. He is mentioned in the Bible as a Priest of the Most High. In esoteric philosophy, He is the King and Father of the planet Earth and the Priest of the Ineffable One, or the One whose Name is Silence, being called by the same Name.

According to ancient legends of Judaism and early Christianity, Melchizedek establishes the right to the manifestation of a special and ideal dignity and extraordinary priesthood, germane to both royalty and high priests. Melchizedek is the prototype of the Messiah. He is the head of eternal angels, and He is "King of peace; without father, without mother, without descent, having neither beginning of days, nor end of life; but made like unto the Son of God; abideth a priest continually" (Heb. 7: 2–3). Jesus Christ was "called of God a high priest after the order of Melchizedek" (Heb. 5:10).

In the ancient Melchizedekian teaching, it was asserted that Melchizedek was the first and principal incarnation of the Supreme God, while Christ was only the image of Melchizedek. It was believed that Christ had descended upon a man, Jesus, at his baptism, and that Melchizedek was a Heavenly Power, higher than Christ. According to their teachings, Melchizedek did for Angels what Christ was to do for people.

The last incarnation of Melchizedek was about 6,000 years ago as the first Zoroaster, or Zarathustra, the founder of Zoroastrianism and a prophet. He was given the Revelation of Ahura Mazda, or the Creator, in the form of the holy scripture of the Avesta in the language of Zend, which is very close to the language of Senzar.

According to linguistic studies, the name *Zoroaster* may be translated as "the golden shining star" or "Golden Sirius". In Zoroastrianism, Sirius is especially revered, being called *Tishtrya*, "whom Ahura Mazda has established as a lord and overseer above all stars, in the same way as he has established Zarathustra above men." Only thirteen incarnations of Zarathustra's have been revealed to humanity, and in each of them was given a sacred scripture which over time was lost, requiring the manifestation of a new cycle of secret knowledge.

The image of Melchizedek bears within itself a seal of High Mystery, and the main pages from His incarnations on the earthly plane, as well as on the Ethereal one, may be slightly opened, but only to those who have ascended the first rungs of Initiation.

**Monad** (*Greek*, "unity") — the fiery seed of the spirit, a Divine Spark, which is eternally reincarnated, clothing itself in various forms; a particle of the One Divine Principle in each manifestation of the world.

It is indestructible, unchangeable, and eternal. It is the same for all existence as the unconscious basis of life. As a particle of the Divine Principle, this spark of life is inseparably linked with this Principle. Its programme includes an aspiration to cognizing Divine Love and the eternal self-perfection of the forms it animates.

Besides, at the dawn of the Grand Cycle of Evolution, every seed of the spirit is begotten under the rays of a specific star or planet, which has its own Planetary Spirit, or Regent. Therefore, the Seed contains the same energies as this Spirit; in essence, the Lord of this star may be called the true Guardian Angel of the monads conceived in His

Rays, and the celestial body itself can be considered to be their Guiding Star for the whole Cycle. All seeds engendered here are part of His own essence, although its vehicle — the human beings for whom He is Teacher and Cosmic Father — may never become aware of this fact. Similarly, the Great Masters of Wisdom have their Father, who has His own Lord, and so on — however, everything in the Universe is indissolubly connected with the Unknowable Divine Principle, who is the Primal Progenitor of all creation.

The more developed the monad, the more advanced forms it embodies itself in. The levels of perfection correspond to the levels of the development of consciousness and are attained by an incredibly long evolutionary process. At the end of the Grand Cycle of Evolution, the Divine Spark returns to its Source, or point of origin, to begin a new cycle of development at a higher level. And so on *ad infinitum*, with neither beginning nor end.

The monad is actually a duad: the union of Atma (*Sanskrit*, "spirit") and Buddhi (*Sanskrit*, "soul"). It is reincarnated in the lower Kingdoms of Nature — mineral, vegetable, animal — and gradually proceeds through them to humanity, clothing itself in appropriate forms. But upon entering the Human Kingdom, the principle of the higher consciousness, Manas (*Sanskrit*, "mind"), joins the duad, forming the divine triad. It is Manas that transforms human beings into rational and moral individuals, and this is what distinguishes them from ordinary animals.

Sixty billion seeds were sown on the planet Earth, bearing the divine triad. All of them belong to the rays of various stars and planets, although they are all on the same temporary stop — the planet Earth. Of course, only eight billion are now incarnated in physical human form, while others are in the Subtle and Fiery Spheres surrounding the planet.

The divine triad is in the human heart. From this fiery seed germinates a special Flame, whose tongues create what looks like the folded petals of a Lotus. The higher the spirituality and morality of an individual, the brighter and stronger will be the radiations of their heart's Flame. As a rule, there are three tongues, or petals, of the Flame — hence the threefold Flame. While there are twelve petals in all, only nine are able to unfold on the Earth and in the current Solar System. The first three petals are green, or emerald, the next three are rose, or scarlet, while the last ones are white. When people receive knowledge, the first three green petals of their heart-Lotuses start to unfold. When they begin to love, then comes the time of the rose-coloured petals. Then appear the last three, the white ones, only of such a colour that is not accessible to the human eye.

Among humanity the vast majority are people with green petals of Knowledge, unfolded in varying degree. The rose petals of Love are revealed in a mere handful of people around the world — people who have reached the level of holiness. The white petals are possessed only by those who work with the Lords — the Adepts and the Initiates.

**Nemes** — the royal headdress of the pharaoh in Ancient Egypt.

**Nineveh** (*Akkadian*) — the capital of Assyria, where one of the largest and oldest libraries was located. The destruction of it, along with the burning of the Library of Alexandria, has deprived humanity of the true knowledge of its past.

**Osarseph** (*Greek*) — the name given to one of the best known priests of Ancient Egypt, who changed his name to Moses. "Moses" should not even be considered as a name, being simply a Judean nickname signifying "saved from the water."

Some researchers erroneously identify Osarseph with the great Jewish prophet Moses, who united into one nation the Israeli tribes and organized the exodus of Jews from Ancient Egypt. Helena Roerich said that Moses must be included in the chain of Names of Mahatma Morya.

**Osiris** (*Egyptian*) — the ancient Egyptian God of resurrection and the afterlife.

**Pallas** (*Greek*) — the name of the area where the Sanctuary of Pelion was located.

**Pallas Athena** (*Greek*) — the ancient Greek Goddess of Wisdom.

**Pelion** (*Greek*) — a mountain in Greece.

**Pillars of Hercules** — the name used in ancient times to denote the heights flanking the entrance to the Strait of Gibraltar.

**Pluto** — the ninth planet of the Solar System, which is actually a large asteroid, or fragment, from a planet that perished in the previous Manvantara, wherein Uranus was the Central Sun. In the records of Helena Roerich, this destroyed planet is referred to as the Best Planet. It has also been named by scientists after Phæthon, the son of the sun god Helios in Greek mythology, who tried to drive his father's solar chariot with disastrous consequences, and was eventually destroyed by Zeus' lightning.

The planet Phæthon died in a collision with a bolide, forming the asteroid belt that is now located between

Mars and Jupiter. This happened because of the destructive activities of Lucifer, which resulted in the debauchery and violation of the Cosmic Laws among the population of the planet reaching its apogee — this left the Comic Justice no other choice but to destroy it in order to preserve the other planets of the system.

The Best Planet had a Progenitor: the Eternal and Immortal, manifested in a unique way as the Creation of the Heart of Infinity — the One Source of all Life unfolding in the Fiery Worlds. If one cosmic body perishes, then another structure arises with the use of new elements, along with those that disintegrated into primary particles as a result of collisions, explosions, superflares, and so on.

As in the great, so in the small — and vice versa. While the quaternary of a human being may have turned into dust and ashes and his spirit created a new human flesh, likewise, the spirit of the Best Planet has given birth to a new cosmic body, which is now located outside the Solar System. Thus, it is possible to see the reflection of the Cosmic Laws both in the great and the small, for in the Universe everything evolves, flowing from one form into another, and these forms can be completely different in appearance (fragments, bolides, planets, stars, comets, and so on), having both visible and invisible forms.

They can also receive those names with which the continuation of the solution of unresolved tasks is associated, such as Pluto or the same Pallas, which is the provisional name of the geographical point where the Sanctuary of Pelion was located in Greece. Various rays were focused on this Point of Life. Another example is the very large asteroid Pallas, which is located in the main asteroid belt between Jupiter and Mars. Despite the fact that it was discovered in 1802 (although it was indicated as a star in Messier's *Catalogue of Nebulæ and Star Clusters* in 1779), it was named after the daughter of Triton and Athena — Pallas. Thales of Argos had studied it since time immemorial as the minor planet Pallas.

**Pralaya** (*Sanskrit*, "dissolution") — a period of rest, or collapse of life within a planet, system, galaxy, or the Universe between various Cycles of Evolution. It is equivalent in duration to *Manvantara*.

**Poseidonis** (*Greek*) — the last island of Atlantis, which submerged below the waterline in 9564 BCE.

**Quaternary** — the four lower bodies of the sevenfold structure of the human being, namely: the physical body, the energy body, the etheric double (the lower astral body), and the emotional-mental body (the higher astral body).

**Ra** (*Egyptian*) — the ancient Egyptian Supreme God, as well as the personalized Sun.

**Race** — a stage in the evolution of humanity. Belonging to various Races is first of all determined by the level of spirituality, or by the coefficient of brightness of the heart — a coefficient termed *Argo*. There are Seven Races in total, each of which has seven sub-races. Each Race develops a particular side or quality in people, densifying or rarefying the matter of their bodies.

People in the first two Races, as well as in the first half of the Third Race, did not have physical bodies — their bodies were of ethereal matter. Those people were genderless beings, not endowed with reason and never dying, for they did not have flesh. They had existed for 300 million years.

Eighteen million years ago, in the middle of the Third Race — i.e., the Lemurians — the separation of the sexes took place, and people began to conceive their progeny.

Humanity received dense physical bodies and began to reflect the Supreme Mind.

The Fourth Race — the Atlanteans — came into being approximately 4–5 million years ago. But only three sub-races of the Atlanteans evolved on the continent of Atlantis while the remaining four were in Egypt, Asia, and Europe.

The current Fifth Race, known as the Aryan, originated about one million years ago in India. In the 20th century the term *Aryan*, as well as additional secret knowledge previously revealed by the Messengers of Light, was used by the dark forces to develop and circulate their anti-evolutionary theories. The Fifth Race's people are now to be found on each existing continent and all its seven sub-races have already formed. Nevertheless, the Third and Fourth Races are still represented on the Earth, too.

The formation of future Races does not require the millions of years needed by previous Races. Therefore, it may be said that the Sixth and Seventh Races will exist and develop simultaneously. Thus, since the beginning of the 20th century, in each country there have appeared the best and most spiritual and moral people, who are generating the next, or Sixth, Race. They are no different from others in their outward appearance, but they have loving hearts, strong energy, and often many abilities and talents. And in the present days the seeds of the Seventh Race are already showing themselves. At the end of this Race, many things that are now considered miraculous will become common, and the attenuation of the human body, as well as the matter of the planet, will reach the point prescribed by the Evolution for this Round and its last Race.

The farther one looks back into humanity's past, the more one can see of its future, for the past contains a projection of the future. Thus the first Races were

143

ethereal — and matter slowly became solid. The last Races will be the same, but this time the matter will gradually rarefy. The end and the beginning are similar in form but distinct in expression. While the beginning was characterized by the absence of self-consciousness, the end is the pinnacle of self-awareness. The middle of the Fourth Round — the middle of the Fourth Race — marks the lowest point of the fall into matter, the densification of the human body, and the development of intelligence. The Fifth Race is on an ascending arc. Therefore, gradually the spiritual must achieve an ever-increasing preponderance over the material and the heart over the intellect, so that by the end of the Seventh Race matter is completely subordinate to spirit to the extent accessible to the Fourth Round of Evolution.

Humanity currently lives in a period of great responsibility — the time of the change of Races. This process is always accompanied by an extremely powerful influence of the Cosmic Fire, leading to a change in the inclination of the Earth's axis and magnetic poles, attended by natural disasters and climate change. Additionally, humanity is reaping what it has sown over this period of its development. As the time of the change of Races approaches, information is being imparted to the world (within permissible limits) through the Messengers of Light, with the aim of warning humanity of the forthcoming dramatic and earth-shaking changes.

Thus, Helena Blavatsky's works and *The Mahatma Letters*, along with other ancient writings, point out that during the change of Races, such continents as America and Europe are to be shaken by powerful earthquakes and submerge into the sea. Edgar Cayce, too, foresaw this scenario for the end of the 20th century. However, the development and collective will of humanity enabled the Hierarchy of Light to prevent such devastating cataclysms. But even they have the right to interfere in such cases only up to 50%; otherwise, humanity will learn nothing. The other half of efforts for salvation are to be made by Earth-dwellers themselves.

America and Europe may have a most beautiful future. Everything depends on people who must keep pace with Evolution, and that requires a revival of spirituality. Also it should be borne in mind that books, films, and other works of art which proclaim yet another "end-of-the-world" scenario and various cataclysms, promote — through human will — thought-forms that take on enormous proportions. Such energies may explode in space, resulting in huge disasters. So, North America finds itself on the Subtle Plane in a rather unstable condition since its population in the Physical World is constantly destroying its own cities and the entire continent — by the thought-forms contained, for example, in its entertainment films, which are distributed worldwide. It requires a tremendous effort on the part of all the colleagues of the Great Brotherhood to prevent such thoughts and the destruction they depict from coming true in reality. But it is also within the power of any conscientious citizen of any country. If someone can erect giant destructive structures simply through their thoughts, then by the same token a light-bearing individual is able to produce creative and positive currents — for example, by prayerful appeals to the Forces of the Light. And then the transfiguring Fire will descend into the lower spheres and mitigate the destructive influence of these negative formations.

Therefore, the manner in which the change of Races will actually take place depends upon everyone: whether through conscious evolution without tragic consequences or through constant upheavals.

**Red Race** — the third sub-race of the Atlanteans, also known as the Toltecs. It was during this period that Atlantis reached its greatest prosperity.

**Sadducees** (*Hebrew*) — an ancient Jewish religious sect. Sadducees held high positions, such as, for example, chief priests and judges, and were known to be fanatical and cruel in complying with their priestly laws. The Sadducees and their followers persecuted the early Christians.

**Sanhedrin** (*Greek*, "assembly") — the highest body of political, religious, and legal authority in Judea.

**Selene** (*Greek*, "Moon") — the Moon; the ancient Greek Goddess of the Moon.

**Sistrum** (*Greek*) — a sacred musical instrument used in the temples of Ancient Egypt to produce magnetic currents and sounds through the combination of its metals. It was used to oust the dark forces, purify the air, and invoke elemental forces.

This instrument was usually made of bronze but sometimes of gold or silver. It had an open circular form, with a handle, and four wires passed through holes, to the end of which jingling pieces of metal were attached. Its top was ornamented with a figure of Isis or Hathor.

**Sons of Life** — in the esoteric tradition, the name given to the representatives of various groups of Ethereal beings — for example, the Seraphs. They can be incarnated in human bodies, yet they do not live a human life, remaining virgins — these are usually monks, hermits, and so on.

The Sons of Life are sometimes called the Sons of Heaven — those who descended to the Earth, being Messengers of Distant Worlds.

However, Seraphs, Angels, and similar beings represent completely separate lines of evolution, and their tasks do not include being Teachers or Masters for Humanity. Whereas the role of a Teacher may be filled by a Spirit who has come from the Distant Worlds, or a human being — a creation of the Earth who has attained the level of an Earthly Master.

**Tartarus** (*Greek*) — in ancient Greek mythology, the deepest abyss, a place of absolute darkness.

**Thebes** — the Greek name for one of the capitals of Ancient Egypt, Waset, which was situated on both banks of the Nile River. Here now, though only on the eastern shore of the Nile, is to be found the city of Luxor.

Near Thebes is the Valley of the Kings, or the Valley of the Dead, wherein the pharaohs of Ancient Egypt (including Ramesses the Great and Tutankhamun) were buried.

In Thebes was the Theban Sanctuary, also known as the Brotherhood of Luxor.

**Third eye** — the organ of subtle plane, which is closely related to the centre of the heart, enabling its owner to see spiritually without the restrictions of Time and Space.

**Titans** (*Greek*) — a race of giants of divine origin in Greek mythology.

Legends of the Battle of the Titans, or the Battle of the Gods, exist all over the world, telling about the time when a group of Gods opposed one dominant God. In fact, these myths reflect the events of the rebellion of the Sons of Light, the Titans of Shambhala, against the dictatorship of Lucifer and his evil sorcerers, which took place when the last islands of Atlantis remained, but the time of the current Fifth Race had already arrived. Compared with present-day human beings, the Atlanteans, like the first sub-races of the Fifth Race, were giants, as recorded in the legends. The victory of the Light over the warlock-giants of the last island of Atlantis, Poseidonis, occurred in 9564 BCE, when it plunged into the water.

The Titans also represent the so-called transitional link from human beings to Gods; that is, these are no longer people, but not yet Gods in the highest sense of the word.

The Titans of the Earth are accorded a separate history in the evolution of the planet, since before the appearance of the first physical humanity, she tried several times to create it on her own. Thus, a few "versions" of humanity followed one another, until the planet realized that without the Help of the Supreme Forces, her own experiments would not lead to anything good. However, in each of her experiments, it was possible to select one or several individuals who had shown the ability to evolve further. It was from their number that the Titans of the Earth appeared.

Whereas the Titans of other planets in the Solar System have their own stages of development (which may be entirely different from earthly conditions), the proportion of the elemental forces on various cosmic bodies may feature different *constants of sound* — or established basic values. These, as a rule, do not change, since they contain fundamental properties of matter and laws of Nature (in this case, of those Worlds which are represented by the Titans). But the most significant influence on the Earth has been exerted by the Titans who arrived from other solar systems, as well as other planetary chains, such as the constellations of Orion, Alpha Centauri, the Pleiades, and others.

As for the constellation of Canis Major, particularly the star named Sirius, here all who were at the level of Titans have attained the rung of Gods, and have descended into the Solar System through the star Betelgeuse, where they were joined by the Titans nurtured by the Gods of Sirius to an almost godlike state.

The Lords of the four corners of the world relied on those who were clearly subdivided into four sectors: the Titans of the North, the Titans of the South, the Titans of the East, and the Titans of the West. These were separate groups of spirits linked with specific heavenly orbs.

**Tlavatli** — the second sub-race of the Atlanteans.

**Triad** — the three higher bodies of the sevenfold structure of the human being, namely: the Supreme Mind, Soul, and Spirit.

**Triangle** — since ancient times the triangle has been endowed with a profound symbolism. The equilateral triangle was called divine, as in it was embodied the sacred harmony of the Cosmos. The isosceles variety was termed demonic as, despite its apparent outward harmony, it was flawed (according to the ancient Greek philosopher Xenocrates of Chalcedon). On the other hand, the scalene triangle reflected the imperfection of human nature and was human.

Subsequently, in different religions, the triangle had a different interpretation — for example, in Hinduism it was a symbol of woman's "animal" force. Thus, representatives of different areas, being in various geographic parts of the world, turned to sacred geometry, choosing the symbol that best corresponded to their worldviews.

Sanctuaries of the Triangle were created mainly by the Sons of Heaven, who had access to the knowledge in the domain of the energy movement of celestial orbs, which on the Earth were designed to "rely" on three points. They also called themselves the Sons of the Triangle, as well as those who later joined their ranks, honouring the Triangle as a symbol of the creation of the Cosmos.

**Underground Fire** — the energy of low-frequency sound, which is often referred to as *satanic*. However, it is such only on the lowest level, bearing disharmonious and destructive frequencies that are the source generating poisonous gas — or so-called "brown gas." The Earth has been likened to a giant cemetery, permeated with the "spirit of decomposition," and at the same time on the Ethereal level she can represent the Paradise Garden.

The gradation of earthly currents is extremely different, presenting itself as both a "weapon of mass destruction" and something like the elixir of life in the form of a certain alchemical substance at the level of its fiery elements. Thus, the forces of evil employ the "unmanifested in spirit" mass of destructive property that may result in epidemics of madness and other cataclysms, not only at the level of consciousness, but also in the spheres of elemental phenomena (earthquakes, volcanic eruptions, tsunamis, tornadoes, global wildfires, floods, and other incidents in Nature — everything related to the manifestation of powerful destructive forces). As to the Forces of Light, they co-operate with the planet at a higher level, searching for those elements that can save the entire sublunary world from gigantic disasters — and eventually bestow currents of Immortality upon the Earth.

**Ur** (*Chaldean*, "Light," "Fire") — a city in Babylonia, where the main Lunar Sanctuary was located; the birthplace of Abraham, the forefather of the Jewish people.

# *Notes*

**1.** Mitar Tarabich (1829–1899), a prominent Serbian prophet, foresaw for the second half of the 20<sup>th</sup> century and present time:

"Among the people of a nation there in the North, a little human being will emerge as out of water and he will teach people about love and friendliness. But there will be many hypocrites and Judases around him and he will have many ups and downs. Not one of these hypocrites will want to know what real human grace is, but his wise books will remain and all the words he will say, and then people will see how self-deceived they were."

Dragoljub Golubović and Dejan Malenković, *Kremansko proročanstvo* [The Kremna Prophecies] (Beograd: Bata, 1990), p. 184.

**2.** Edgar Cayce (1877–1945), a famous American prophet, predicted that new religious ideas would come from Russia:

"For changes are coming, this may be sure — an evolution, or revolution in the ideas of religious thought. The basis of it for the world will eventually come out of Russia; not communism, no! But rather that which is the basis of the same, as the Christ taught — His kind of communism!" (29 November 1932)

"Out of Russia, you see, there may come that which may be the basis of a more worldwide religious thought or trend." (25 August 1933)

"In Russia there comes the hope of the world, not as that sometimes termed of the Communistic, of the Bolshevistic; no. But freedom, freedom! That each man will live for his fellow man!" (22 June 1944)

Edgar Cayce, *The Complete Edgar Cayce Readings* (Virginia Beach, VA: A.R.E. Press, 2006), CD-ROM, Readings 452–6, 3976–12, 3976–29.

**3.** In 1978, Vanga (1911–1996), a renowned Bulgarian prophetess, predicted that the New Teaching of the White Brotherhood would appear in Russia in 1998:

"The New Teaching will come from Russia. That country will be the first to be purged. The White Brotherhood will spread across Russia and from there its Teaching will begin its march throughout the world. This will happen in twenty years — it will not happen earlier. In twenty years, you will reap the first rich harvest."

Zheni Kostadinova, *Vanga* (Moscow: AST, 1998), pp. 71–72.

**4.** A year before her departure, Helena Roerich (1879–1955), the author of the *Agni Yoga* series, who continued the mission of Helena Blavatsky, warned that her work would be continued by the next disciple at the end of the 20th century:

"It is also necessary to pass on the foundations of the Fiery Experience. Many people at the end of our century will come to it, and one of the Sisters of the Brotherhood will be my successor, and she will carry out Agni Yoga under new and, possibly, improved conditions." (10 October 1954)

Helena Roerich, *Pis'ma* [Letters], vol. 9 (Moscow: Mezhdunarodnyi tsentr Rerikhov, 2009), p. 468.

## *Other Titles Published by Radiant Books*

### The Teaching of the Heart series

- The Call of the Heart (2016)
- The Illumination of the Heart (2016)
- The Heart of the Community (2017)
- The Heart of Infinity (2017)
- The Fiery Hierarchy (2017)
- The Fiery Heart (2018)
- The World of Fire (2018)
- The Prayer of the Heart (2018)
- Brotherhood (2019)
- The Sun of Love (2019)
- The Joy of the Heart (2020)
- The Rainbow of Fire (2020)
- The Fruit of Love (2020)

**The Book of Secret Wisdom (2015)**
**Parables from Shambhala (2016)**
**The Secret Book of Dzyan (2018)**
**The Ascending Goddess (2020)**

Printed in Great Britain
by Amazon